SUSAN WITHIN

WHEN A PAST LIFE RETURNS

S. M. HARRIS

TOP CAT PUBLISHING

ISBN: 9798994608593

CONTENTS

Prologue 1
1. The Remembering 3
2. A Decree of Silence 7
3. Waking Up to What? 13
4. The Voice 19
5. The Tadpole Years 22
6. The Music Was Always There 27
7. Eleven Months 30
8. The Gift is You 35
9. The Light of My Life 43
10. Another Springtime 50
11. A Thread Between Souls 57
12. The Perfect Door: A Story Rewritten 63
13. Vanity's Last Stand 69
14. Susan? Who's Susan? 74
15. The Black Sleeves 78
16. Perfectly Out of Place 84
17. The Job That Set Me Free 87
18. "If It Breaks, Can You Fix It?" 92
19. Just Ask 97
20. A Reunion Across Lifetimes 102
21. When Two Lifetimes Met 106
22. The Day Normal Disappeared 110
23. One Small Miracle at a Time 115
24. The Promise Unfolds 120
25. Kip in the Spotlight 124
26. Happy Dreams 130
27. A New Direction 135
28. Into the Arts 140

29. It's All Love 146
30. Ivory 152
31. Winter's Gift 155

About the Author 161
If You Enjoyed This Book 163
Continue the Journey 165
Books by Sally M. Harris 167

PROLOGUE

My adventure began when I was nine years old.

"Your daughter has viral pneumonia," the doctor had said.

My parents brought me home and tucked me into bed.

I tried to read a book, but the words blurred. I coughed and felt weak. My chest ached. Then I got very hot. Too hot. I called for my mom, who was always in the kitchen doing something. This time, both parents came in. My fever had spiked. My mom placed her cool hand on my forehead.

"She's burning up!" she said.

I can still picture their expressions: alarmed, caring, and completely present. But I was strangely at peace. In my nine-year-old mind, I wasn't afraid. I'd been sick before and had always gotten better.

Then something happened.

Suddenly, I was no longer in my body. I was up in the corner of the ceiling, looking down.

I saw my parents leaning over my small frame, brown pixie-cut hair damp from illness, surrounded by sunny yellow walls, dolls, seashells on doilies, and ceramic cats lined up on the dresser.

And just as suddenly, I was back in my body, back in bed, with my parents still hovering over me.

"I just saw myself from up there," I told them, pointing. They looked at each other.

"We'd better get her to the doctor right now," my dad said. He scooped me up and carried me to the car. It was winter. I remember the cold air, sharp and bracing.

At the clinic, the doctor said, "You're lucky. The cold air brought down her fever. No need to admit her to the hospital."

We went home, relieved. But something had shifted. I remembered being soul, free from a body. But I was just a child, and no one spoke of such things. So I didn't.

I tucked it away. But it left me with the gift of an open, curious mind, and a sense that life held more than what my physical eyes could see.

1

THE REMEMBERING

It started with a book my brother handed me, like it was no big deal.

"You've got to read this, Sally. It'll rock your Mormon world."

I read the first two pages, and something in me broke open.

I was a fifth-generation Mormon; my ancestors on both sides of my family were pioneers who followed founders Joseph Smith and Brigham Young. I loved God and Jesus, taught Sunday school, and worked in the church nursery. But the dogma and male hierarchy never felt like home.

I sometimes wondered if that meant I wasn't destined for the highest level of heaven. And since I often leaned on my own ideas instead of the priesthood's, I knew that could put me at odds with church authority. Still, I cherished the members' kindness, and

I stayed because of the children. Their wide eyes and sticky hands made every Sunday worth it. I'd show up with a felt storyboard or a fresh batch of homemade play dough, and they'd dive in with such joy you'd think I'd brought treasure.

I'd never been a "spiritual seeker." I hadn't read Carlos Castaneda or wandered into New Thought teachings. But the book my brother gave me changed everything. It spoke of soul travel, of consciousness beyond time and space. It described a personal journey toward spiritual awakening and how anyone could access that same experience themselves.

It spoke of the Light and Sound of God not as metaphor, but as a reality that could be seen and heard within. Not with eyes or ears, but with an inner knowing. Where my religion had offered structure and certainty, this offered a luminous path to spiritual freedom.

By the second page, I wasn't reading anymore. I was remembering. It was a sacred language I already knew.

I felt an aliveness within me, something vast and familiar, a presence I would later call soul.

For the first time in this lifetime, I sensed true freedom. Each word felt like a reunion, like joy returning from a place it had waited patiently.

I carried the book with me everywhere—between chores, late at night, in the car. I even read while baking chocolate chip cookies for my husband and son. Good thing the oven had a timer, otherwise those cookies would have been casualties of my awakening.

Much later, my husband said something I never forgot: “I always knew I married you too young. Before you discovered who you were.”

He was right. I was working part time in a dental office and going to college, convinced I was laying the groundwork for a safe, steady future, duplicating my parents’ lives. But the more I read, the more I felt I had been dozing through my existence.

With that awakening came an ache I didn’t expect. If the book were true, what did that mean about everything I’d been taught? I longed for my family’s acceptance, but I feared my new joy might look like betrayal to them.

When I finally told my mom I was leaving the Church, she broke down in tears. We were at the kitchen table where every important family conversation happened.

She'd been snapping green beans into a colander, and her hands suddenly stilled.

"I don't want you to go to hell."

The beans sat forgotten. Her fingers, still garden-dirty from the morning, trembled against the table's edge. I was the eldest daughter of five kids, much older than the little ones playing in the next room. They looked up to me. I could see in her face that she wasn't just afraid for my soul, she was afraid my choice would ripple through the whole family, pulling them away from everything she'd built her life upon.

Her fears never came to pass. In time, she even confided that she believed she was a reincarnated pioneer. And one by one, each of my siblings chose their own path, just as I had.

I came to understand there is a spiritual path for everyone, and soul is drawn to the one that matches its level of awareness.

But back then, the landscape of my life was shifting overnight. I started having vivid dreams of flying, of moving from one place to another with only a thought. Or I would see things the night before and watch them unfold the next day. I had always sensed things, but this was different. The rules I'd been taught no longer applied.

The Mormon Church, which had once shaped my world, now felt distant, like a house I'd lived in but never truly owned. I was leaving a plain vanilla world for one of vibrant flavors, each one surprising, alive, and waiting to be explored.

2

A DECREE OF SILENCE

I tried to share my new experiences with my husband, but I didn't know how. We were only in our twenties. He seemed content with sports and chasing the American dream. I was a dreamer of another kind.

I went to church alone with our son while he stayed home and watched Sunday football.

It wasn't a surprise that we couldn't communicate on a spiritual level. Although we appeared to be a perfectly matched young couple, we shared very little actual connection.

A year earlier, my family doctor had noticed a change in my demeanor and asked me about my marriage. I was speechless when tears welled in my eyes at his questions. He handed me a business card for a marriage counselor, as seriously as if he were writing a prescription.

My husband refused to go. Months went by before I asked again. I had been depressed for too long. His answer was still no. He said he'd had enough psychology in college and considered himself his own best counselor.

The constant tension was too much, so I decided to stay with a friend for a week to sort things out. She had experienced spiritual awakenings of her own, and with her, I felt safe.

I called my little boy every night, told him I loved him, and promised I'd be home soon.

My husband was a man I trusted. A former elementary school teacher, now a firefighter and fire inspector for the city, I thought he would understand that a short break might help.

When I returned after that week, I was even more confused. I didn't know where I belonged. For that one week, I had been with someone who understood me. The depression and loneliness felt lighter when I was away. Now they returned heavier than ever. Our situation had become serious, and I told my husband I didn't know what the future held.

He didn't get angry. He just looked at me for a long time and said, "You've changed."

There was no argument. Just a silence that said everything.

Finally, he said, "If you decide to leave me, no court in the world will give you custody of our son. You abandoned us." And in that moment, something in me froze. I believed him because he worked with the mayor, and I assumed he knew the law. I didn't dare leave him.

After a year of trying to make things work, I finally left in early December. I took only a few belongings. My plan was to come back for my son once I was settled. I didn't want to uproot him until I could offer stability.

I had nothing. I even sold my Mercury dime collection for gas money. My grandfather had given it to me when I was a girl, and my husband handed me fifteen dollars for the entire set, all he was willing to offer, knowing I was broke.

I scooped up the stray cat I'd been feeding, put him in my 1962 Dodge Dart, and drove away while my son watched from the window. It was the most painful moment of my life.

That first night, I slept in my car at a rest stop.

Eventually, I found a tiny apartment and moved in. Alone, it felt stark and soulless. I quit school, let go of my dream, and tried to survive. Then came the legal papers—mounds of depositions from my husband's family and friends, many of whom barely knew me. Some of it read like bad fiction; the rest like a courtroom soap opera.

On Christmas Eve, divorce papers arrived at my door.

My hands shook as I held the papers. I had eaten toast for dinner three nights in a row and had thirteen dollars in my checking account. If I fought this, I'd need a lawyer I couldn't afford. If I didn't fight, I'd lose my son. My throat tightened.

There was only one chair in the living room and a tiny Christmas tree in the corner, lit with soft, blinking lights. But when I read the papers, something inside me gave way. I picked up the little tree, carried it outside, and dropped it into the dumpster. To this day, Christmas trees remind me of that moment.

~

HER OFFICE SMELLED like old coffee and copy toner. I sat in a green vinyl chair that squeaked when I shifted my weight. The lawyer I'd found at the last minute—the only one I could afford—sat across from me, her pregnant belly pressing against the edge of the desk.

I may have imagined it, but I sensed a bit of judgment from this young mother-to-be. Maybe it was in her eyes, or in the way she slid the papers toward me, barely glancing at them.

"I'll be taking maternity leave soon," she said, almost apologetically. "But we can amend this later. This is just a starting point."

I believed her.

I lifted the pen, a cheap ballpoint with her name on it, and signed away my rights.

~

THE FINAL DECREE was made in a courtroom I never entered. There was no court hearing. Papers were signed behind closed doors. Somewhere, a gavel may have fallen.

All I knew was the result.

I was granted joint custody, but with an outrageous condition. The decree stated that if I shared my spiritual beliefs with my son, if I used words like *reincarnation*, *past lives*, or even discussed my *dreams*, I would immediately lose all parental rights.

Later, my husband told me he knew the judge and hinted that the decree had been granted as a personal favor.

It was a violation of freedom of speech, entered into law by a judge who should have known better. That was the moment I stopped believing the system would protect me.

I complied. Until my son was eighteen, I censored myself, afraid that one slip would cost me the right to see him. The decree of silence pressed down on me like a vise, treating me as a criminal for what I believed. Each time I dropped my son off at his father's house, I knew he would be asked what I had said and whether my beliefs had come up. The thought of my son being questioned like that broke my heart.

I went from teaching little children in Sunday school about God's love to being forbidden to speak of God to my own son. All I could do was pray in silence, reminding myself that somehow, in ways I couldn't yet see, all was in order. At times, I felt the presence of an angel, or perhaps a spiritual guide, or even a beloved relative, wrapping me in love, offering encouragement. My spiritual life grew rich even as my outer life crumbled.

Looking back, I choose to believe no one meant to be cruel. My ex-husband thought he was protecting our son. His family believed they were standing beside him. Somewhere along the way, I stopped being a person and became a symbol of something that threatened their world.

They did not understand the language I had begun to speak—the language of dreams, intuition, and past lives.

But even as my outer freedom was bound by a decree, another freedom was quietly unfolding within me.

A freedom no judge could limit. The freedom of soul.

3

WAKING UP TO WHAT?

I was beginning to sense that soul awakening isn't one-size-fits-all. We each have our own timeline, and mine came with detours, plot twists, and divine breadcrumbs that didn't always make sense.

It would be years before I had a complete picture. But I knew this much: my soon-to-be ex-husband and I were no longer on the same path. His road looked paved, straight, predictable, sensible, and perfectly acceptable. Like a well-worn path lined with streetlights and speed-limit signs. Safe, but uninspired.

Mine? Mine looked like it veered off into the forest with a hand-painted sign that read:

"Warning: Spiritual Growth Ahead. Bring Snacks."

One day, before the ink dried on the actual divorce agreement, I answered the door to find the bishop from the Mormon Church I used to attend. I had a feeling my soon-to-be ex had sent him in a last-ditch attempt to win me back, or maybe just to frighten me into compliance.

But the timing was perfect. I'd been wondering how to get my name removed from the church membership list. I'd heard you had to notify headquarters in Salt Lake City, and the bishop's visit saved me the trouble.

He was a kind-faced, balding man who looked as if he carried the weight of the world on his sloped shoulders. He said solemnly, "Sally, I'm here about your membership. I hear you've not been abiding by the principles of the Church. We want you back, but first, you'll need to attend a disciplinary council for excommunication. After a period of repentance, you can rejoin the Church and again partake of the sacrament on Sundays."

My reaction was probably not what he expected.

"Thank you, Bishop," I said. "I'm so glad you came today, because I've been wondering how to remove my name from the church records. If you could take care of that for me, I'd be so grateful."

He frowned, bowed his head, and quietly took his leave.

I closed the door and stood there for a moment, letting it sink in. Leaving the Mormon Church wasn't just leaving a religion—it meant stepping away from everything I'd been taught about eternal families and the highest level of heaven. I had been told that by walking away, I might lose my place with my loved ones in the next life.

And yet, deep down, I knew that wasn't true. I had already begun to unlearn the conditioning and remember the deeper truth that lived beneath it.

I felt free. I was grounded in the path I'd chosen and no longer ruled by fear, only anticipation for the glorious adventure ahead, despite the unknown.

I thought of Robert Frost's poem "*The Road Not Taken*"—and those famous lines:

> "I took the one less traveled by,
> And that has made all the difference."

It had made a difference, yes, but not without a cost.

I was learning to trust the divine, to listen to spirit. But I was still a mom who was denied ordinary days of parenting.

I missed school lunches, scraped knees, and night-time hugs. No mantra, no affirmation, no prayer could reach the place inside me that grieved.

I tried to get my son back full-time. I'd followed my lawyer's advice. But she never mentioned I needed to challenge the divorce decree within the first year. She just said we could amend the agreement later.

"Just a starting point," she'd told me.

I believed her. But by the time I went to another lawyer, I found out the door had locked behind me, and no one had left a key under the mat.

I went to three lawyers over the next year. Different offices, same conversation. They'd read the agreement, frown, and spout some version of: 'Unless there's documented abuse...' or 'The window to change the decree has closed.' It didn't matter that I had a safe home or a deep bond with my son. When the reality sank in that I was stuck with the custody arrangement, I had to adapt.

Work helped. I loved my job as a dental assistant and built lasting friendships with both staff and patients.

The dental office became more than a workplace—it became the backdrop for a spiritual experience...

One night, my friend Karen called me at home, frantic with a toothache. "What can I do, Sally? I know it's after hours, but I'm going crazy with pain!"

From her symptoms, I knew it was an abscess. I gave her my boss's home number and wished her luck. When I went to bed, I didn't know if she'd reached him or if he'd gone in to help.

That night, I had the most vivid dream.

I was in the dental clinic, standing unseen beside the treatment chair. Karen sat in it, mouth open. The doctor leaned over her, and searched through the instruments in frustration.

He was trying to find the right tool, a reamer, one of those slender, colorful files we used to open up an infected pulp chamber. But the tooth's canal was too narrow. Nothing fit.

I watched him leave the room and head to the hallway drawer. He rummaged around and pulled out a red-handled reamer—one I'd never seen him use before—and returned.

As I stood beside him, watching, I felt calm and completely present. The whole experience had a clarity to it, like I was there to witness something important, even sacred.

It felt real. But when I woke up, I told myself it was just a dream.

The next morning I went to work and noticed the treatment room was a mess from the night before. Karen *had* come in.

And on the tray, sitting exactly where I'd seen it in the dream, was the red-handled reamer.

"What happened here last night?" I asked the doctor.

He rubbed his eyes. "I couldn't get into the canal—had to dig through the hallway cabinet for something small enough. Found that little red reamer, and it worked. Sorry about the mess. I was beat."

I just stood there, staring at the tray. It hadn't just been a dream.

I'd been exploring soul travel, learning that some dreams are more than dreams. They're visits, departures, glimpses from somewhere just outside the body, beyond space and time.

I should've sterilized that red reamer and tucked it into my pocket—a sacred souvenir from that night.

It felt like the start of something new. A confirmation that I was exactly where I needed to be, even when it hurt.

4

THE VOICE

Looking back on those years—through the chaos, upheaval, and pain—I can see now that a deeper order was at work. Every twist and heartbreak belonged to it. Nothing was random. They were soul appointments.

Does that sound like I'm justifying things? Maybe. Minimizing consequences? Possibly. But here's what still amazes me. I was warned. Forewarned that something would separate my son and me.

I remember the moment clearly.

I was standing in the bedroom of our townhouse, holding my sweet two-year-old son balanced on my left hip the way I always carried him. He could walk by then, but I loved having him close, his small arms looped around my neck, his warm cheek resting against my shoulder.

Sunlight streamed through the window, filling the

room with a soft afternoon glow that made everything feel safe and ordinary. A pile of freshly folded laundry sat on the bed.

It was a perfectly normal moment.

Until it wasn't.

The room grew oddly still, as if the air itself had taken a breath.

And then I heard it.

A voice, calm, firm, and deeply familiar, spoke.

"When he is five, you will not be with him as you are now."

I looked around. I knew we were alone in the house. But I also knew the voice had not come from outside. It came from somewhere inside me.

The words landed with a weight I felt but could not explain. I did not fully understand them, but I recognized their origin.

It felt otherworldly.

Not a threat. Not even a warning in the usual sense.

I was strangely calm. That surprised me. Shaken, but not afraid. Mostly, I was stunned to hear that message, especially when my journey as a mother had only just begun.

I could not imagine a world without my son.

My arms tightened around him. He squirmed, wanting to get down and play, so I let him slide to the floor and watched him toddle toward his toys.

I told myself it meant something harmless—maybe

I'd go back to work when he started kindergarten. Maybe it meant nothing at all.

But I knew better. The voice carried the weight of fate, not possibility.

I was twenty-four, and my world still felt like a sweet ride. Being handed a future like that was too much, so I told no one. After all, what would I say? How do you speak of a prophecy that promises to break your heart?

I tucked it away and moved on. And it was not until after the divorce that the message came rushing back.

When the memory returned, it was a salve on an open wound. I finally understood the voice hadn't come to frighten me. It had been preparing me.

Even then, I was not alone.

5

THE TADPOLE YEARS

The years that followed brought blessings, hard lessons, and the slow working out of old karma.

Back then, I was a tadpole in a spiritual pond, sensitive, curious, and a little wobbly. But I was all in.

The first thing that grabbed me was the law of cause and effect. What I thought, what I said, what I believed—all of it had power. My energy didn't just float around harmlessly. It rippled. And let's just say... I was making quite a few waves.

I used to joke that I must've signed up for the fast track at karma school. Like someone in the spiritual admissions office had stamped my file: Expedited burn-off required. The lessons came quickly, sometimes wrapped in grace, sometimes in grit, but each one chipped away at old layers and helped me remember who I was.

A big part of my tadpole curriculum was reincarnation. I had already been given a preview course when I was sixteen.

I walked into the auditorium wearing my miniskirt and chunky platform shoes, happy for a break from history class. A movie in the middle of the school day was always a treat, even if it was supposed to be educational.

The old projector had sputtered to life, the reel clicking as it turned. A black-and-white Nazi symbol flickered across the screen, grainy and ominous. The chatter in the room faded as my classmates and I realized what we were in for. It was the Holocaust.

I'd seen photographs and a few old newsreels before, but this was different. Maybe it was the feeling of being packed into a crowded auditorium that triggered what happened next.

Suddenly, I wasn't just watching anymore.

I was there.

I closed my eyes. The smell hit me first: unwashed bodies, sickness. Then the sounds—distant screams, barking dogs, the slow shuffle of feet with nowhere left to go.

I felt the hunger, the exhaustion, and the numbness that comes when people stop expecting tomorrow to be better.

I wanted nothing to do with it. I slammed the door shut in my mind and locked it tight. If past lives existed,

I didn't want to know. I didn't want to believe I'd really been there.

Years later, when I delved into spirituality, reading about reincarnation was fine. But I was about to meet it head-on when I met a man from Würzburg, Germany.

His name was Uwe, but he went by David. He looked a lot like Sylvester Stallone. No kidding. I had actually dreamed of someone who looked just like him a few nights before we met, which naturally made me think it was a sign.

He was charming, but I felt uneasy in his presence, especially when he spoke German. A chill ran through me whenever I heard it. I'm half German myself, but something about hearing it now made me want to crawl out of my skin.

And yet there was a magnetic pull between us I couldn't explain. I wanted to believe my dream of David meant destiny, not danger.

David talked me into getting married right away. He was a car salesman who made marriage sound like a great idea. When I hesitated, he closed the deal with a smooth line and a salesman's smile, then handed me the keys.

My son liked him. David had played on a German soccer team and offered enthusiastic coaching. On holidays, I received luscious chocolate from my mother-in-law in Germany. What could be better?

Those were the best parts of the relationship. But underneath, a dark current was brewing.

For years, I'd had occasional nightmares carrying the same horror as the film I'd seen in high school—scenes from a concentration camp. I never spoke of them because I didn't want to believe they were anything more than my imagination.

After marrying David, the nightmares grew more frequent and intense. Then one night a nightmare unfolded like a full-length horror movie, complete with barbed wire, smoke, hollow faces, and hopelessness. I woke up drenched in sweat.

But this time I didn't slam the door, because by then I'd gained some spiritual tools and grown some tadpole backbone. Enough to stay present, at least.

I closed my eyes and meditated on the scene, replaying it over and over. This time I stayed calm, watching it from a distance with compassion instead of fear. Then I wrapped it in love and let it go.

After meditating, I knew I'd been given another chance at life—a different kind of life this time around. For that, I was grateful.

Facing that lifetime from World War II freed me. Now, the sound of the German language only reminds me of what my ancestors sounded like.

But healing old wounds didn't mean I'd stopped walking into new ones.

What I didn't understand at first was how much David drank, and how, once he'd had enough German beer, a darker side emerged.

It began with raised voices and flashes of temper.

Eventually it became punched doors and broken walls.

David never revealed that side of himself to my son. But one night, when we were alone, he put his hands around my throat and made it clear how much power he believed he had. "I could kill you if I wanted to," he said.

My whole body went cold, and in that instant, the illusion of love shattered.

I had to get out.

Our connection had one clear purpose: to bring that old soul memory to the surface so I could finally face it.

Leaving him was one of the first times my little spiritual tadpole grew legs. I wasn't just floating in ideas about karma and healing anymore; I was using them to walk myself out the door.

After our relationship ended, I sat on the floor and closed my eyes. I was exhausted, raw, and strangely clear. I remember silently asking for help to show me what was next.

And then I had an extraordinary out-of-body experience.

6

THE MUSIC WAS ALWAYS THERE

The karma had burned off like fog in the morning sun. And yet I was in no-man's-land, knowing where I'd been, with no map for what came next.

From that in-between space, I tried a spiritual exercise I had learned.

I leaned against the wall in the condo hallway, slid to the floor, and sank into the soft tan carpet. I closed my eyes and took a few cleansing breaths to steady myself. My focus shifted to that sweet spot between my eyebrows, known as the third eye.

I chanted a word I'd learned: HU, a simple sound, like a sigh shaped into prayer. Two letters, one syllable, said to be an ancient name for God. Softly at first, then with growing confidence, I let the sound carry me beyond the walls of that hallway.

I chanted for a couple of minutes, just long enough

to quiet the monkey brain—the endless chatter that kicks in the second I try to meditate.

Suddenly, I was soaring in a black, starlit night.

Oh my gosh—I'm moving!

I was heading somewhere. Clusters of stars streaked past me in every direction, glowing and shifting like rivers of light. And then I heard it. A flute playing the most beautiful melody. The notes seemed to come from just ahead, as if it were leading me, calling me forward through a vast sea of stars. It felt like it was around me, even inside me.

The flute didn't sound like any instrument I'd ever heard. Each note was light as air, yet full of presence, as if it had its own intelligence. Some tones were high and bright; others hovered low and warm, like a memory you couldn't quite place. The music invited me to move with it, as if it knew the way home.

I flew past the stars so fast it felt like the entire universe was rushing by. Some shimmered with steady light; others drifted like clouds of silvery mist.

I knew I could keep going. I was moving forward with purpose. I couldn't see my body, but I sensed it.

I followed the sound, softly singing HU as I went. It was freedom—ecstasy, beauty, and awe beyond anything I'd ever known.

Was I just imagining it?

The moment I began to analyze it, I was flung back into my body, the return swift and elastic, like a rubber band snapping home. It was over.

It wasn't the first time I'd experienced something beyond ordinary reality. But it was the first time it had happened while I was fully awake, fully conscious.

Was it real? I can't tell you what happened in any scientific sense. All I know is that my body still remembers the sensation of moving through those stars. My heart still hears that flute.

But something had changed. I now knew other worlds and dimensions existed alongside this one—hidden in plain sight.

That flight through the stars confirmed what I had long suspected: there was far more to explore.

7

ELEVEN MONTHS

Travelling through the cosmic spheres was amazing. It gave me a glimpse of a reality beyond time and space. But soon after that experience I had to face the physical consequences of the unconstitutional divorce decree.

I had been careful to hold up my end, making sure not to talk about religion in front of my son.

Then one day a friend—with a big red Cadillac, a huge head of curly hair, and an even bigger mouth—made a mistake. He knew about my decree, but he casually mentioned reincarnation in front of my son.

I remember the moment. My friend was yammering on about a book and he suddenly mentioned past lives. I turned around to look at my son, who was sitting in the back seat. My heart did a little flip when I saw him frown. I knew it bothered him. In truth, I don't think he liked my friend.

He was in fifth grade, caught between two parents. For reasons I may never know, he repeated the forbidden word to his dad. I'm sure he had no idea what would come of it.

My ex seized on it as proof that I was breaking the terms of the custody agreement, and he took matters into his own hands. He had remarried and made it clear he didn't want me in our son's life.

I did not know how far he would actually go.

When I drove over to pick up my son, I got out of the car and waited for him to come running, his backpack bouncing the way it always did.

Instead, my ex rushed out of the house, crossed his arms, and yelled, "You just lost custody!"

I stood there, stunned. "What? I'm here to pick up my son."

"You talked about reincarnation. You just lost custody," he repeated.

I couldn't move, couldn't talk.

When he refused to let me see my child, I stumbled back to the car and drove away, too numb to even cry.

What he did next set the legal system in motion. My ex hired a lawyer who served me with a document claiming I had failed to pick up my son ninety-one times.

My jaw dropped open.

In truth, there had only been one time when the schedule got confused, after my ex had switched days with me so he could go on vacation.

I wasn't sure whether his wife had come up with this or whether he had grown more creative in his storytelling. Either way, ninety-one missed weekends and weekdays would have required me to disappear for nearly two years—something I'm fairly certain I would have remembered.

The document was a smokescreen for what he really wanted: me out of the picture.

Probably because of his outrageous claim, the court appointed a child psychologist to sort truth from fiction and evaluate our son's emotional state. The process took eleven long months. I never knew why, but I suspect my ex wanted to drag it out as long as possible.

During that time, I was forbidden to see my child. In my heart, I knew only the love I had for him and the deep injustice of what was happening.

One day, I stood outside his elementary school during recess, my hands wrapped around the chain-link fence, peering through it at the playground.

Children ran and shouted, their laughter carrying across the schoolyard. I searched every small face before the bell rang, hoping for a glimpse of my son.

But I couldn't call out to him. I couldn't even wave.

He never knew I was there.

I was not allowed to contact him. Not even a phone call was permitted.

A familiar ache rose inside me. It reminded me of when my son was born and immediately whisked from my arms and placed in an incubator. I longed to see him, but my legs were too numb from the anesthesia and I couldn't walk.

Now, once again, he had been ripped away from me, this time by his father and the court system.

It was a nightmare. Without my son, work became the center of my universe. Yet I couldn't confide in anyone there because I was afraid they wouldn't understand, or worse, judge me. Most of them assumed my son lived with me full-time. I never said anything different because in those years there was a stigma if you didn't have full custody. I needed to fit in and appear "normal."

Each day I worked on patients and mingled with coworkers, smiling on the outside.

After signing the divorce decree, my life was already under a microscope. Silence and discernment became my shield.

~

ELEVEN MONTHS after my ex denied me access to my son, I finally got a court date.

The judge scowled as he read the child psychologist's report, then pointed at my ex and said, with a thump of his gavel, "Give Sally her son back immediately. And pay all her attorney fees."

He reinstated my custody because I was not the

person who had mentioned the forbidden word: reincarnation.

When the nightmare was over, my whole body relaxed. My son was coming home.

I had no idea that my struggle would soon bring someone remarkable into my life.

8

THE GIFT IS YOU

My life was a song, shifting between melodies. Some days it sounded like the Beatles' *Let It Be*. Other days, it was *Bridge Over Troubled Water*, and I carried those lyrics in my heart:

> Oh, if you need a friend
> I'm sailing right behind
> Like a bridge over troubled water
> I will ease your mind.

I longed for companionship. I wanted a man with whom I could share my spiritual journey, a fellow explorer with a kind heart and humility. It sounded like a tall order, but I knew he was out there.

Ironically, my lousy divorce decree became the unlikely path that led me to him.

The custody decree still contained the religious clause. I wanted it removed, but I was barely making ends meet. I had already sold my Buffet clarinet just to pay the last lawyer.

Finally, I confided in a trusted friend.

"Call Al Harris," he said. "He's a professional musician, but he also has a law degree."

I had heard of Al and had even seen him on stage, a jazz pianist who played at seminars I attended.

So I phoned him.

But to my dismay, he couldn't help me because his law degree was from Canada.

Still, we chatted a couple more times until there was nothing left to discuss about my legal matters. Then, just as I was about to say goodbye, he surprised me.

"I'd like to take you out for dinner sometime. Would that be okay?"

"Sure. But why don't you come over for a home-cooked meal instead?"

For reasons I didn't yet understand, I wanted Al to come to my apartment. I had just decorated the walls with colorful bamboo and silk fans, and it felt important that he see my simple Zen-like furnishings, even though that style was new to me.

He arrived with slightly wilted grocery-store tulips.

"Sorry," he said, holding them up with a sheepish grin. "The roses looked like they were having a worse day than these guys."

I liked him immediately.

Al was a few inches taller than me, with wavy dark hair and a moustache left over from the seventies. His pianist's hands gestured as he talked, slender fingers punctuating the air, unmarked by the calluses of labor.

He touched one of the silk fans on my wall. "This is beautiful."

Then he looked at me with deep brown eyes. "Do you know about wabi-sabi?"

"No. What's that?"

"It's Japanese—finding beauty in imperfection."

He smiled, with a slow warmth that crinkled the corners of his eyes. "Like these tulips."

I found myself laughing, something I hadn't done easily in months.

After dinner, he took me for a drive in his little white Yugo, an economy car many people found amusing. He pulled out his driving glasses, placed them on his nose, and glanced over at me.

"I've had these forever. I call them my Buddy Holly glasses!"

I couldn't help laughing. They were the nerdiest things I'd ever seen.

I learned that he had studied Japanese in university, traveled in Japan, and was a black belt in karate.

We started dating.

I would like to say everything was amazing, like soulmates reuniting in joy and bliss. But it was not. Both of us had unfinished business.

A pattern slowly emerged, like an old-time photo

developing in chemicals. At a party with his musician friends, I stood slightly apart, and waited for him to include me in conversations. When he introduced me, I bowed my head slightly, a gesture that startled me when I realized what I was doing.

The strangest moment struck me when we were walking down a Seattle sidewalk. I'd unconsciously positioned myself three steps behind him.

When he stopped to look in a shop window, I bumped into a parking meter because I hadn't been watching where I was going—I'd been watching him. I'd wanted a partnership, but I was behaving like a follower. Strange, because that was not who I was.

Meanwhile, Al was facing his own dilemma, which I only learned about later. His old girlfriend had put their relationship on hold, calling it a break. That left him free to date me, or so it appeared. I tried to guard my heart, careful not to fall too fast.

One evening, while I was home alone practicing with a newly acquired eBay clarinet, a powerful vision interrupted the music.

The apartment was dark except for one lamp. As I played, I thought of Al, and suddenly I heard piano chords, as clear as if someone were playing in the next room. I lowered the clarinet and the music stopped. My heart was pounding.

I closed my eyes, and the vision continued, like a movie projected onto my eyelids. Al and I were in a sun-filled house, his hands fingering piano keys while I played clarinet beside him. The scene shifted to a garden, my hands patting the soil at the base of a flower, while he brought me tea. Another shift—a circle of friends gathered in our home, all of us laughing together.

I was overwhelmed by a feeling of purpose, partnership, and joy. This was my future. I could feel it.

Then the phone rang and the vision faded.

It was Al.

"My girlfriend told me she wants us to be together again," he mumbled. "I won't be seeing you anymore, Sally."

I squeezed my eyes shut and sucked in a sharp breath. The apartment was warm, yet a chill rippled down my neck and I shivered.

The room went strangely still.

A dark curtain of blood poured down before me, blocking out everything else. Then another vision pushed through the crimson veil behind it.

I saw Al in another lifetime. The slash of a samurai sword sent him crumbling to the ground. I dropped to my knees beside him, clutching the hand of our two-year-old son. A primal cry tore from my chest, and the pain was so intense I could barely breathe.

And in a flash, I remembered that in this life, Al had an appendectomy scar on his torso. But now I saw it with fresh eyes. It marked the exact spot where the sword had pierced him in my vision.

The pieces were fitting together like parts of a jigsaw.

The vision evaporated and left me alone with the silent phone in my hand and a heart scraped raw with grief.

Why had God given me a preview of a wonderful life if it was not meant to be?

As time passed, I came to understand that we had reunited just long enough for me to allow that past-life memory to surface and heal. Al had been the trigger.

We never could have made it as a couple with that old storyline. That Japanese lifetime needed to be recognized and released. And I needed to create a life of my own, without him.

Or so I thought.

Letting go of Al was one of the hardest things I'd ever done. The months that followed were thick with absence. But I picked up the pieces of my life, something I was getting used to.

~

TWO YEARS later I was days away from making a serious commitment to another man, even though he was not my first choice. But if God did not want me to be with Al, I had to move forward.

Alone in my apartment, I was about to go to sleep when the phone rang.

To my surprise, it was Al.

"Hi. I was thinking of you, Sally. Want to meet me for some pie and coffee?"

It was ten o'clock at night. What the heck. I said yes.

We met at a restaurant, and I immediately felt at ease in a way I hadn't before. The distance was gone.

I wasn't "walking behind him" anymore, I was sitting across from him, fully myself.

We chatted like old friends, and he told me that he and his girlfriend had broken up for good. Strangely, I felt detached. There was no agenda, no desperate hope. Just two people having coffee.

He asked if we could see each other again. I said yes, as friends, because I was seeing someone.

But each time we met, it became obvious that we were meant to be more than friends.

I ended things with the man I'd been dating, because I could no longer deny my feelings for Al. The moment I let my boyfriend go, it was as if the heavens opened.

Wherever Al and I went, even in public places, the world seemed to step aside. We were always alone. It was magic.

Spirit was arranging the details. Together, we were twice the light, twice the joy. Ours was a connection that spanned time—familiar, sacred, eternal.

One day, we were walking by ourselves in the University of Washington Arboretum, surrounded by summer flowers and lush green trees. Koi circled beneath lily pads in a nearby Japanese garden. Al squeezed my hand and stopped me.

"Close your eyes for a second."

We stood there together, the summer sun warm on our faces. I could hear water trickling over stones, birds in the trees, and the distant sound of traffic on the boulevard.

"I'm getting something," Al whispered. His voice was soft, almost reverent. "A message from Spirit."

I kept my eyes closed, barely breathing.

"It's asking me a question: 'If God put a gift in front of your face, would you accept it?'"

There was a moment of silence.

"The gift is you, Sally," he said, and pulled me toward him. "You're my gift. And I'm saying yes."

Tears spilled down my cheeks, but I was smiling.

If I had learned anything, it was this: the wheel of karma keeps turning whether we are ready or not. I had chosen the road less traveled, and my vehicle showed it. A few dents. A cracked windshield or two. The occasional warning light blinking for reasons no mechanic could explain.

Still, there I was. Keys in the ignition. Wondering what the next stretch of road might require.

9

THE LIGHT OF MY LIFE

On paper, we made no sense at all.

Al was Canadian. I loved the U.S.A.

He had never had kids or cats. I had a son and two Siamese.

He loved jazz. I preferred rock and roll.

He went to law school but as soon as he graduated he started a music production company. That was who Al was. Dedicated. Willing to follow his heart.

Sometimes I wondered why he found me so interesting.

I just worked in a dental office.

And yet, we moved in together.

He set up his music studio in the spare room, and for the first time I watched how he worked—composing and producing, filling our home with creativity and joyful sound. It echoed the vision I had carried inside me of the life we would share.

Living together brought new growth. And with new growth came a new perspective in the form of a lens.

One afternoon, Al approached me, hands behind his back, grinning like a kid with a secret.

"Close your eyes," he said.

"Al—"

"Just do it."

I closed them. Something heavy and cool settled into my palms—metal, glass, the faint smell of leather.

"Okay, open your eyes."

I looked down at a Canon AE-1, its silver body worn smooth with age. The lens cap dangled from a cord.

"Al, I can't—this is yours."

"Was mine. Now it's yours."

He sat on the edge of the bed, studying me.

"You know what I see when I watch you? Someone who notices things. The way light comes through the kitchen window. The way a bird pauses on the fence before it flies. You already see like a photographer, Sally. You just need the tools of the trade."

"I don't know the first thing about—"

"So learn." He adjusted the strap on my shoulder. "Your son's nearly grown. You've spent years taking care of everyone else. Now it's your turn."

I stared at the Canon, a manual film camera full of dials and decisions. It was 1990. Digital photography hadn't arrived yet, and neither had YouTube or online tutorials.

I DIDN'T KNOW if I could actually learn photography, but I enrolled in a class at a local college. I learned the basics from an eighty-two-year-old woman named Fern Kennedy, and then signed up for her night photography class.

Just days before Christmas, we bundled ourselves up, grabbed our tripods, and headed to Bellevue Square to photograph the lights. Fern arrived with a huge thermos of hot cocoa and poured each of us a cup. As she moved among the students, her laughter rang out in the frosty air, and I thought, *I want to be just like her*.

Even now, when I point my camera at Christmas lights, the aurora borealis, or a moonrise, I replay that evening in my mind, re-experiencing the excitement of that first time photographing in the dark. In a way, I bring her with me.

Fern inspired all her students. "Sally," she said. "If you ever make it into international competitions, it would be a feather in your cap." I didn't really need a feather or a cap, but it gave me something to reach for.

Fern's husband, a retired court judge, quietly supported her. Each week he brought in charts to help us understand photography. Watching the two of them work side-by-side, I glimpsed what partnership could look like as it deepens with age.

That, too, was a gift—perhaps as important as the class itself. Mentors often show you more than you expect. Witnessing their ease and respect for each other gave me something I hadn't realized I was missing: hope, and a blueprint for the life I was building with Al.

After a few classes, I'd gotten pretty good at flower photography, and Al noted that. When he suggested a trip to Hawaii to photograph exotic flowers, I should have been thrilled. But I was more wary than happy.

It was hardly the reaction he expected, yet he was still excited to show me Hawaii, since I'd never been there before.

He made arrangements to produce a radio jingle for a travel agency in return for five-star accommodations at Poipu Beach on the Garden Island of Kauai, an all-expenses-paid, first-class vacation.

Al produced the jingle, and I packed our bags.

We spent Christmas Day with friends in Hanalei, and they took us to a nearby heiau, an ancient Hawaiian temple and sacred site. Everyone was excited to go except me. Since I'd arrived on the island, I'd been in a strange mood, unable to shake a growing sense of fear.

At the heiau, I wandered off by myself, stood at the edge of a cliff and gazed down at the cobalt-blue sea as waves crashed against the black rocks far below. The color was deep and mesmerizing, both beautiful and haunting. Behind me, a stone ledge rose from the ground. I stared at it and shivered. Then I closed my eyes and began to softly sing HU, my breath rising and falling with the rhythm of the ocean.

A vision arrived.

I WAS A YOUNG GIRL, maybe twelve. The sun beat at my face, but I couldn't close my eyes. Someone had painted them, and the paint stung.

Rough hands clamped my shoulders and pushed me forward.

The ocean below was the same cobalt blue, but the air tasted different—humid, heavy with salt, and filled with terror.

I heard chanting in a language I didn't know but somehow understood. Singing to the gods.

Singing me toward the cliff edge.

My heart hammered against my ribs like a trapped bird, and my mouth opened in a silent scream.

More hands pushed me. And then there was only air...and water.

Frozen with fear, I remembered to keep chanting HU—and kept chanting until the fear softened.

Then the vision fractured and dissolved, like sea foam breaking against stone.

Slowly, I opened my eyes, and I was present again. The surrounding colors seemed brighter, and I understood that I'd been shown something from another lifetime—and been given the chance to heal it.

Later, our friends confirmed what I had sensed: the site had been used for human sacrifice.

From that moment on, the energy shifted, and whatever had lingered from that ancient lifetime was gone. I began photographing the island's vibrant flowers with my trusty Canon AE-1, and suddenly beauty was everywhere.

~

TWO YEARS LATER, Al and I decided to get married. Before we'd met, I'd seen photos of friends exchanging vows at sunrise on Maui and that's what I'd wanted.

It was December and we headed for the Seattle airport, skidding down the freeway through a foot of snow and ice.

My parents were coming too. A few months earlier my dad had been diagnosed with leukemia, and we were still reeling from the news. But he was determined to do as much as he could. True to his adventurous spirit, he drove through the heavy snow to reach the airport, and they caught the last flight out before SeaTac shut down.

On the morning of our wedding, I awoke at 3:00 a.m. and wondered where everyone was. I'd forgotten to change my alarm to the new time zone. I was a little too early for our sunrise wedding, but far too excited to go back to sleep.

When I put on my wedding dress around 5:30 a.m., I glanced in the mirror and caught sight of a woman with unruly hair and tired eyes. It wasn't the bride I'd imagined I'd be, but she was the one who had shown up.

As the sky lightened, Al drove us to the beach in Wailea. When we arrived, I stepped out of the car, paused, and breathed in the ocean air.

Our friends from Kauai arrived with gifts: they placed a flower garland on my head and a fragrant ti leaf lei around my neck. In that moment everything shifted. As the flowers touched me, I absorbed the love surrounding us. The ocean glowed with soft pink light, and the morning turned sacred.

I felt like an islander, wearing a wreath of baby roses and satin ribbons woven by a kahuna, a traditional Hawaiian healer. Al and I both wore sweet-smelling plumeria, and the scent of blossoms surrounded us.

Hand in hand, we stood barefoot in the sand.

Looking into Al's eyes, I said: "You are the light of my world, and I will treat you justly at all times." In return, he spoke the same vow to me.

My dream wedding had manifested because of that earlier trip to the heiau on Kauai, where a past-life trauma was finally brought to light and laid to rest.

The wisdom of soul amazes me. It knows what must be healed.

And another healing was just around the corner.

10

ANOTHER SPRINGTIME

Timing doesn't always look divine. It can look like a sterile room and a sudden diagnosis.

I was newly married, and life was good. Then came Valentine's Day.

The doctor looked up from my chart and said, "I'm afraid you've got some abnormal cells. We need to do a biopsy now."

There was no time to react. The procedure began immediately—unexpected, invasive, and sharp enough to pierce more than just skin. Afterward, I slipped off the table, dressed, and drove seven miles through rush-hour traffic, hands unsteady, heart trembling. My husband met me at the door and guided me to the dining room table, where I sat in stunned silence, staring at nothing.

It was several minutes before I could speak, and

when I did, my words, "probably cancer," were barely audible.

How long I sat there, I don't know. The truth jarred me awake: my body was a fragile vessel, an hourglass with sand running low. It felt as though I had awakened from a long sleep of aimless dreaming.

It was time to get down to business. Of course, I had no idea what that business was. I simply began noticing life more closely, as if seeing through a macro lens. Every detail shimmered. Every moment mattered.

Weeks passed. I focused on healing, both body and spirit. And the lens remained, zoomed in on life's offerings.

Then, one early spring morning, around 4 a.m., I awoke with words in my head.

I flipped on the light, grabbed a pencil, and scribbled them down, the first few lines of a poem. I turned off the light and apologized to my husband for disturbing his sleep.

Five minutes later, another verse came.

They arrived like newborn kittens, one by one, until the poem was finished by sunrise.

The oddest part? I had never written poetry before. And this one was perfect, needing no editing except for one word: *forevermore*.

It sounded like something from the 1800s, so I changed it. It would be years before I discovered why that word had appeared in the poem.

Another Springtime

It's now another springtime
As she looks into the mirror
That shows so many seasons
And days of yesteryear

The birds outside are singing
Songs she's heard before
How many years, she wonders
Will spring knock at her door?

It's now another springtime
The world outside is new
She knows that she is aging
And only passing through

An inner voice is whispering
"Your time is almost here"
With memories of love inside
She has but little fear

It's now another springtime
With promises to be
For her, it is the season
When love will set her free.

The next morning, poem freshly printed and in hand, I headed to work. That single sheet of green paper with its floral border and hopeful lines was about to touch many lives.

My boss, a tall, good-natured dentist, encouraged creativity, even in a world of tooth extractions and fillings. I was just beginning flower photography, and he let me hang my prints in the patient rooms.

I showed him the poem.

"This is great!" he said. "Go hang it up in the waiting room!"

I blinked. The waiting room? I wasn't sure I was ready for that kind of exposure.

But I did it. That morning, I pinned *Another Springtime* to the bulletin board.

It was April 1994. I remember the timing clearly, not just because it was my first poem, but because of what happened at the office the day I hung it up. If I ever forget when I wrote it, I just have to look up the date of Kurt Cobain's death. He had died two weeks earlier, and grief was still thick in the air, especially here in the Pacific Northwest.

To my surprise, two of the remaining members of Nirvana were scheduled as new patients. That afternoon, Krist Novoselic and his wife Shelli arrived for their appointments. David Grohl was set to come in the next day.

They entered through the front door like anyone else. No entourage, no fanfare. We treated everyone the same, with kindness and professionalism.

I grabbed Shelli's chart and stepped into the waiting

room. “Hi, Shelli—it’s your turn!” I said with my usual smile. I always tried to put our patients at ease. I understood dental anxiety all too well.

But instead of following me back, Shelli paused and pointed to the wall.

“Who wrote this poem? I’d love a copy, if that’s okay.”

“I did,” I answered. “I’d be happy to make you a copy. In fact, I just hung it up this morning!”

I looked into her pretty, young face. Her eyes were brimming with tears.

“You probably know our other band member, Kurt, died just two weeks ago. We’re having a rough time. I really like your poem. It says just what I needed to hear right now.”

I thanked her, and we walked back to the treatment room together. She sat down quietly.

It was a soul-to-soul moment for both of us. Her grief and vulnerability had opened a space, and somehow the poem filled it. She felt the love behind the words. She knew it, and I knew it.

There was time to chat. I’d taken the X-rays and was waiting for the dentist. Shelli noticed the photography on the wall.

“These are amazing! The colors of the sea and the flower photos go really well together,” she said. I was glad to be talking about something happy, and soon she settled in and smiled.

“I’m a photographer too,” she said. “I like black and

white and have been experimenting with Polaroid over the last few years."

"Cool!" I replied.

"If you want," she continued, "I can bring you the album of Polaroids from when the band was just getting started. Most of them are from the old garage they used to play in, back when we lived in Aberdeen."

On her next appointment, Shelli brought the album, thick, worn, and packed full of Polaroids. She kept it on her lap as we waited for the dentist, and I sat beside her, carefully turning the pages.

They were all there: candid glimpses of the band in its earliest days. Grainy black-and-white shots of Kurt, Krist, and David in a dimly lit garage, guitars slung low, faces open and unguarded. The raw energy was unmistakable. Each image was a time capsule from their humble beginnings in Aberdeen.

As I flipped through the pages, I felt a mix of awe and intimacy. These weren't just photographs. They were windows into the spark of something that would later shape a generation. Holding them felt surreal.

I thought of my husband, a professional jazz musician. I'm familiar with the behind-the-scenes world of rehearsals and late-night gigs, the bond among bandmates. Still, there was something deeply personal in those photos, a purity of purpose, a fire just starting to catch.

Right then, I felt an unexpected kinship with their journey.

Looking back, I imagine that moment was healing for Shelli. As we sat together, revisiting those Polaroids, it might have brought her back to simpler times—before the world knew their names, before the headlines and heavy demands. Back to when it was just musicians in a garage, chasing a dream. Those photos held more than memories. They held a kind of grace, evidence of where it all began and, maybe, a small comfort in remembering the love and joy that came before the loss.

Surrounded by fading Polaroids and the hum of the dental office, we held a silent vigil. No words were spoken, yet the weight of remembrance hung heavy. Through shared glances and unspoken understanding, we honored Kurt's memory, letting the images say what our voices could not.

I hadn't expected much from a simple poem on a bulletin board. But that day I learned that when we offer what flows through us, Spirit can use it. Even the smallest creation can become a lifeline, offering comfort, opening hearts, and reminding someone they're not alone.

11

A THREAD BETWEEN SOULS

Life carried on after *Another Springtime*, but I began noticing patterns—small synchronicities and perfect timing.

On a rainy afternoon, a new patient named Rinda strolled into the dental office like a haiku: quiet, clever, and completely unexpected.

I found her in the waiting room, reading my poem on the wall.

"Hi, Rinda, come on back! I'm Sally. Nice to meet you," I said with a smile.

She stood tall, not from height but from inner grace. Delicate as a bird, with sparkling eyes. There was mischief in her smile and a quiet depth behind it, equal parts pixie and old soul.

She held up her arms to show me goosebumps. "Your poem moved me to tears," she said with a grin.

"That's how I know something's true. Goosebumps don't lie."

Then she tilted her head and, with stunning certainty, told me who I was, spiritually and emotionally, as if the poem had revealed me to her. How could she do that?

She reclined in the dental chair, and I fastened the yellow bib around her neck. I noticed how tiny and delicate she was, yet her spirit filled the room. I sensed she might be ill, and she would later confirm that. But in that moment, she felt like a messenger. How was I lucky enough to be seen so clearly by someone I had just met?

I soon discovered she was a poet too, and we became instant friends.

I had a feeling more poetry was coming to me. The first one had arrived in a dream, so I stayed on alert for the next. When it came, I was fully awake, pencil in hand. The verses unfolded in my mind during one of those moments when even my reflection in the mirror seemed unfamiliar. It was as if another voice had joined mine.

The poem explored aging, identity, and timeless beauty, and I couldn't wait to share it.

"I'll give it the goosebump test," Rinda said over the phone.

I read it to her, and it passed.

On my days off, I'd drive to her place for a beach walk. Her red house sat just steps from the bay, weathered by salt air and time, but it suited her, unpretentious and full of character.

What I remember most is how she came alive outside. She strutted along the coastal trails. Shoulders back, eyes bright, her hair dancing in the breeze. The salty air seemed to charge her spirit. Even the gulls looked like old friends. I saw it in her face, how the outside world brought her to life.

"Come on, Sally! Let's go just a little further. I want to show you something!" she'd call out, already a few steps ahead. It would be a breathtaking view around the bend, or a massive piece of driftwood shaped like something wild. She cherished every inch of the beach.

She had once been a researcher and writer, studying the behavior of seagulls. She didn't just walk the beach; she was intimate with it. It wasn't only a view; it was home. The tides, the gulls, the salt air—they were all part of her.

Illness shaped Rinda's days. Though her father had been a doctor, traditional medicine failed her, so she turned to alternative paths, managing a condition that left her weak. Even so, she glowed, not with health but with a light from somewhere deeper, as if she remembered something the rest of us had forgotten.

For months, she'd asked me to come watch *The Power of the Word*, a Bill Moyers special on PBS about poetry. I kept meaning to, and I thought there would be time.

There wasn't.

The last moment I saw her was three weeks before Christmas. It was a blustery night. I had just finished a long day at work and was ladling out steaming chicken noodle soup when the doorbell rang.

She stood on the doorstep, smiling and breathing in the scent of dinner as if it were sunlight.

"Can I have a bowl of soup?" she asked.

I laughed. "Of course."

She ate slowly, savoring each bite like a gift. Then she handed back the empty bowl and said goodbye.

I had a strange feeling in my bones. The entire visit felt surreal.

I turned to Al and said, "That was odd."

After that night, something shifted. Her voice on the phone turned dreamy, distant. I wondered if she was medicated. I gave her space, thinking it was what she needed.

Looking back, my attention was elsewhere. Work left me little time for friendships. Just days before Christmas, a mutual friend called to say Rinda was gone. She had taken her own life.

I replayed our last visit again and again. Her smile. The soup. The way she lingered in the doorway.

If only I had realized.

I'd known Rinda for less than a year, yet it felt like lifetimes. Even now, thirty years later, I still feel the thread between us, and the grief. I've had close friends, but Rinda was a once-in-a-lifetime friend, and the world feels lonelier without her.

In retrospect, the clues were right in front of me, but I never saw them. They were even in this poem she wrote near the end:

Heaven Bound

There is a place
Inside of me
Where dragons dare not dwell
Where light is all there is to see
And priestesses foretell

Of days to come
When a song of love
Is sung the world around
'Til each and every one of us
On earth lives heaven bound.

Sometimes I wonder if *Another Springtime* was the reason we met, or if we would have found each other anyway. Maybe the poem was a doorway she recognized, something her soul had been waiting for. Maybe mine had too.

Word Play

A poet's
Words are
Butterfly wings

Of light

Set free
To explore
With curious intent

Pausing to rest
On each hilltop of Truth
Sometimes finding kindred souls
Basking there

Nothing in the world
Makes a heart sing like that.

Rinda and I had crossed paths not to change the outcome, but to recognize something eternal in each other.

12

THE PERFECT DOOR: A STORY REWRITTEN

Every wound has a beginning.

I was only twenty when I married my first husband. But I was not the first "Sally" he had loved. His high school sweetheart, Sally Johnson, had broken his heart when she left him for a preacher after graduation. To his family, she was "the one who got away."

It was a story his family often retold at the dinner table.

One night over pot roast and mashed potatoes, the story came up again.

"They were the best couple," my ex–mother-in-law said, reaching for the salt. "I wonder how she's doing. Is she still in California? We sure miss her."

Everyone nodded.

She wasn't angry at Sally for leaving her son, only sorry she was gone.

I shrank low into my chair at those dinners and wondered why the other Sally seemed more loved in their eyes. With each retelling, the comparison sank in deeper. The message was clear. She was their favorite, and I was their second choice.

Young and trusting as I was, I swallowed that story whole.

And it hurt.

Even after I gave them a grandson they would mention her, as if I could never quite measure up.

Years later, when I left that family behind in divorce, I thought I had finally stepped out of the other Sally's shadow. Yet the question lingered: why wasn't I good enough?

What had I done wrong? Or what could I have done differently? Those questions nagged me, unanswered, like a low hum beneath the surface of my life.

Yet Spirit was moving behind the scenes, choreographing a lesson, waiting for the right time to reveal it.

That moment came on an ordinary day, just outside my door.

Al and I lived in a 200-unit townhouse complex in a busy, cosmopolitan city, a place where neighbors came and went and most people kept to themselves. Now and then, I would catch the faint aroma of cooking or hear soft voices through the walls, small hints of lives unfolding behind closed doors. We smiled at neighbors in passing, but rarely knew anyone's names.

We lived mostly anonymous lives until one Saturday

when a garage sale a few miles away set an extraordinary series of events in motion.

I had found a dining room set, exactly what I'd been looking for, but I had no way to get it home. So I drove back to our complex with a hopeful heart and scanned the parking lot for a miracle.

That was when I spotted a white pickup truck parked directly across from our condo.

I took a chance that our neighbors might help us. I walked over and knocked on their door. When it opened, a woman greeted me with a bright, welcoming smile.

"Come on in," she said. The scent of coffee and warm cinnamon drifted from the kitchen. When I asked if she could help transport a dining room set she said, "That's my husband's truck. I'm sure he'll help you out."

I was instantly drawn to her. Her face looked vaguely familiar, though I could not imagine why.

She was around my age, maybe older, with a casual warmth that matched her home. Family photos lined the walls of a comfy living room, the kind that made you want to kick off your shoes and stay a while.

Finally, I'd found a friendly neighbor I could talk to. We had a few minutes to chat before her husband came in, so we exchanged a few personal details.

They had moved up from California a couple of years ago, but she told me she was originally from Edmonds.

Edmonds. That was *my* hometown. "What's your name?" I asked.

"Sally," she said.

I froze.

"Did you go to Edmonds High?" I guessed the year she graduated.

"Yes, I did. That's the year."

"Are you Sally Johnson?"

She laughed. "How did you know?"

I stood there, convinced I had just crossed over into *The Twilight Zone*. "You're the one that got away. I married your high school boyfriend. But I'm not with him anymore. You were the first Sally. I'm the second."

I told her my story. That even after I was married, her photos still filled the walls of my in-law's house, and every time I walked past them, I felt a twist in my stomach.

There she was, Sally Number One, at the prom with my ex, the blond cheerleader and the star quarterback. The wall was a photographic shrine to their young love. And here I was, Sally Number Two, trying for years to earn the warmth his family had already given her.

When I mentioned those pictures to the other Sally, she just laughed and shook her head. "Oh, gosh," she said lightly. "I didn't even know they still had those."

That was it. No drama. No attachment. Just a pleasant memory she had tucked away and moved on from long ago, while I'd been holding onto it all these years.

I realized that I'd been haunted by a ghost who had never existed.

I was still reeling when Sally's husband came downstairs, and something about his solid, kind presence helped me find my footing again.

He carried the same gentle warmth she did. She had found her true mate in this minister.

Before we left to pick up the dining room set, the most unexpected feeling overcame me. Love.

I saw her for who she was: a genuinely joyful, loving person. Of course, my ex and his family had adored her. Any parent would want their son to be with someone like her. And all those years I had felt slighted, comparing myself to the photos on their walls.

Later that day, after the dining room set was safely in place, its polished wood gleaming under the chandelier, I sat down, ran my fingers along the smooth edge of the table, and shook my head in disbelief. Out of 200 doors I could have knocked on, it was Sally Johnson's home. We both lived in a city far from Edmonds, and twenty-two years later, I had found her.

Not just the girl in the prom pictures, but a kind, funny, down-to-earth woman who helped me finally see what I should have known all along. It was never about me not measuring up. It was about her simply being easy to love, and me needing to meet her in person to figure that out.

The "first Sally," my imaginary rival, had welcomed me into her home. And in that moment, she became an emissary of grace, placed gently in my path to soften an old story.

For years, I'd carried the narrative of not being enough. I was well into adulthood before I realized how deeply it had shaped my perception of both myself and others, always wary that they might see the real me with all my shortcomings.

Spirit had gone to a lot of trouble to orchestrate that day with Sally Johnson. As the years went by, I could see it wasn't just to free me from the storyline I carried. It was a turning point.

Almost overnight, I felt a deeper empathy for others, and my mission became clear. My poems and stories were to be inspirational, to come from a place of love and support for the human experience.

When I knocked on the door to meet Sally Johnson, I was really meeting myself for the first time. And in doing so, I began to see others more clearly as Soul. I wanted to shine a beacon of light and truth that illuminated the beauty of who we are. Our interconnectedness and divine nature became the foundation of my work as a writer and photographer.

And if a neighbor ever knocked on my door, I hoped I would remember what that moment had taught me—to greet them with the same kindness and understanding I had finally learned to give myself.

13

VANITY'S LAST STAND

Sometimes we think we have it all figured out. Then the rubber hits the road.

Nothing tests your spiritual growth like losing your address, and that's exactly what happened when we were forced to move from our beautiful condominium into an old mobile home.

I'd thought I'd made peace with the old story about not measuring up, but that move pushed every vanity button in my brain.

After four years in a ritzy neighborhood, we needed to downsize. A dishonest property manager had financially mismanaged our condominium association, and we, along with our neighbors, ended up paying the price.

One morning, I followed a hunch that led us to an older mobile home park. One unit was for sale, and the owners, Bob and Margaret, were desperate to move. Margaret was seriously ill and needed a drier climate.

When I stepped inside, I had to hold my breath. The air was stagnant, and the place felt like a dark cave where time had stopped. The décor was pure 1960s: worn, stained, and slowly disintegrating. But Bob was kind. His only concern was his wife, and he asked for nothing more than moving expenses.

A home for $1,500 was hard to resist, especially when it included brand-new deluxe appliances and a fully equipped workshop. My husband and I looked at each other and agreed it was too good to pass up. We wrote him a check.

It was impossible to miss the irony. The 1962 triple-wide was on multimillion-dollar waterfront property along the shore of Lake Washington. It was a spectacular view. The park had once served as a filming location for an Elvis Presley movie, and I pictured a time when the rows of metal homes were shiny and new, and Elvis was strumming a guitar in someone's driveway.

I loved entertaining friends and family, but suddenly the idea felt inconceivable. Maybe in a couple of years, after we recovered financially, we could move into a "real" home again and resume our social life. Until then, I was too embarrassed to let anyone see how we lived.

I set about repairing and remodeling the mobile home, and for a month, I worked tirelessly to make it livable. But even with new carpet and fresh paint, in my mind it was still an old trailer.

When we finally moved in, something unexpected happened. Our neighbors were warm and friendly. They talked to us, something our former neighbors in the ritzy complex had never done.

Then friends somehow found out where we lived. They stopped by. And they sincerely admired our home.

More people came over in the first month than had visited us in four years at the condo.

Two months later, one final lesson in vanity arrived.

I noticed an offensive odor coming from underneath the mobile home. Around the same time, I read an article in *The Seattle Times* about a man who specialized in odor control. I called him, and he said he would be happy to help.

There was just one catch.

A local TV news crew wanted to feature his next job.

That job was mine.

"Wait... I'm not going to be on TV, am I?" I said.

"Let them come out and talk to you," he said. "You can always say no."

The next morning, Meg O'Conor, a well-known Seattle TV reporter, arrived with a Channel 11 news crew. I'd seen her on TV before. Now she was standing in my living room.

Only then did the reality hit me. This story would air in two states and into Canada. I was about to tell half the Pacific Northwest that I lived in a 1962 mobile home with a horrible smell.

Meg shook my hand. "If you're comfortable, I'd love to ask you a few questions about the odor and how it's affected you."

"I really don't like being on camera," I said.

She smiled. "Just talk to me, not the lens. We'll keep it short, and you'll do great."

I hesitated.

"All right," I heard myself say. "Just a few questions."

At the last minute I wanted to back out. But the writer in me didn't want to disappoint the public.

We filmed for two hours, and when the odor control technician inspected our home, the source of the odor turned out to be rat urine from under the house.

The crew rushed back to the studio to edit, and I waited anxiously for the broadcast.

When the time came, I tuned in to the news. The producers had scheduled my story as the final two-minute human-interest piece.

As the moment approached, I panicked. Thoughts of running away, and worse, flooded my mind.

What had I done?

What had I been thinking?

At the height of my fear, a mirror hanging on the wall beside me suddenly fell and shattered into hundreds of tiny pieces. The mirror had been securely mounted.

As I stared at the shards, an inner voice spoke to me, saying, "It doesn't matter."

But I was on TV for the first time in my life, living in a rat-infested mobile home. Again the panic. Again the voice, this time more emphatic, said, "It doesn't matter."

I began to relax and enjoy the broadcast. The news team had done a great editing job, and the story was actually interesting. I watched myself on TV with a kind of detachment.

I felt like a player on a stage.

Then I realized—that's exactly what I was.

And just like that, vanity packed up and left... right along with the rats.

14

SUSAN? WHO'S SUSAN?

After seven years at the clinic where I wrote *Another Springtime*, I was ready to find a new dental office—a different vibe, a different kind of experience. I left with a smile, a sense of fulfillment, and one last cookie from the break room.

Soon, a Japanese dental clinic hired me to be the office manager. Dr. Lisa, an American-born dentist, had taken over from her Japanese father, who had designed and built the practice himself. She hadn't been out of dental school long, and she appreciated the experience I brought to the office. For the first time, it occurred to me that getting older had its perks.

The space was modern and peaceful, filled with warmth and a sense of legacy. Many of our patients were Japanese. Some were longtime patients of her father; others were professionals from Japan working temporarily in the city at Microsoft.

There was something grounding about it all, a rhythm that made it easy to feel at home. The office was calm, caring, and free of drama. Patients trusted Dr. Lisa's gentle touch.

I loved the pancake restaurant next door. When patients arrived, the scent of butter and maple syrup often followed them in, drifting all the way to my desk like a warm, delicious hello. It was the only dental office I knew that smelled like breakfast instead of disinfectant. By noon, I was usually craving pancakes.

One morning, a patient stepped through the door, paused, and said, "Oh, wow, it smells amazing in here!"

I smiled. "That's our aromatherapy! Fresh pancakes."

"You should hand out menus instead of toothbrushes."

"Don't tempt me," I said. "I've been hungry since 8 a.m."

Outside, a small Japanese garden offered balance with stones, moss, and the soft rustle of bamboo. I felt at peace. Even the trickiest insurance claims seemed to untangle themselves.

I didn't speak Japanese, but I could sense the meaning behind the words. Some of our elderly patients spoke little or no English, yet they would stand at my desk, explaining something in Japanese. It happened often. I listened with different ears, tuning in beyond language. I'd nod, smile, offer a gesture, and it was enough. We understood each other.

At the time, I wore my dark hair in a sleek, blunt cut, and my almond-shaped eyes sometimes drew questions. A few patients asked if I was part Japanese. I wasn't, at least not in this lifetime. As I mentioned earlier, I'd once known Al in Japan, long ago. Perhaps that office stirred something in me, an echo of another time. Sometimes I caught my reflection in the mirror and felt a brief, puzzling sense that I was looking at someone I didn't fully know yet.

There was a Zen simplicity in the clinic that made space for something new. Ideas for poems blossomed like dandelions in spring.

I jotted lines on sticky notes and appointment cards between patients, while sorting insurance codes or trying to remember which Mrs. Tanaka had the bridge on the upper left.

One morning, after a night of writing poetry, a longtime patient walked in, smiled, and said, "Hi, Susan."

I looked up, startled. My nameplate, sitting right in front of me, clearly said *Sally*.

"Sally," I gently corrected.

He paused, blinked, then laughed. "Oh! I knew that."

But his face didn't show the usual awkwardness of someone who'd misspoken. The name Susan had come out on its own.

I laughed it off, but something in me shifted.

After that, it happened a few more times. Always

with people who knew me, and always after I'd written a poem.

Each time it caught me off guard.

It wasn't just a slip of the tongue. The name kept appearing as if someone or something were trying to get my attention. I couldn't ignore it anymore.

I needed a clue. Why did that name keep finding its way to me?

No one was in the waiting room, so I closed my eyes and inwardly sang HU, the sacred name of God I often turned to for guidance.

When I opened my eyes, I glanced down at my arms and froze. They were cloaked in the long black fabric of an old-fashioned dress, edged with a delicate row of white lace at the cuffs. A chill ran through me, and then, just as suddenly, the vision faded. I was back in the present, wearing my white blouse.

I sat there for a long moment, taking it all in. And then, still stunned, unsure of what had just happened, I did the most ordinary thing I could think of.

I went back to filing insurance claims.

15

THE BLACK SLEEVES

What had I seen? The vision replayed in my mind on an endless loop, but I wasn't afraid or uneasy. Mostly, I was curious. I had glimpsed something that didn't belong in the here and now; that much was clear. And when the vision faded, I stood at my desk exactly as before. But I was no longer the same.

No matter what I wore—a sweater, a blouse, a skirt, or slacks—I could feel the brush of a long-sleeved black dress against my skin, as though I wore an invisible garment.

The vision of a woman from the past lingered. Susan. I didn't know more than that.

"Okay, I'm okay...this is good," I said to myself. I told only my husband, no one else. By then I'd learned to keep my spiritual experiences private, to blend in.

Along with my new viewpoint, a common theme

blossomed in my writing: poems and stories centered on the seasons of a woman's life.

In the middle of whatever I was doing, I'd often stop to take "dictation" from an inner voice that was growing stronger and clearer. Words tumbled onto paper, each one becoming a verse or story that needed to be told.

The titles reflected the seasons: from *Summer's Child* to *Winter's Gift, Midlife*, and even a poem about a girl's first menstrual cycle called *Rite of Passage*.

I wondered how it was possible to write about midlife and the winter years before I'd lived them. But somehow I could project ahead and sense what it would be like. I felt driven to describe each one.

I learned to work with angels. When I was stuck, I'd call upon them for help. Guidance came in many forms: a vision, the right word or phrase coming to mind, or my Siamese cat leaping into my lap and purring.

In third grade, my teacher planted the seeds for my writing. I still remember standing beside my mom when she said, "Sally's going to be a writer someday."

What could I possibly have done to give her that impression? She must have been channeling a message from Spirit, or maybe she just mixed me up with another kid. Either way, I believed it and tucked it away in a mental file labeled *something I'll do someday*.

When I finally wrote *Another Springtime*, I realized writing was an important part of this incarnation. I submitted that poem to *The New Times*, a Seattle publication, and they'd accepted it.

The morning it appeared in that newspaper, I couldn't stop smiling. Al and I were having breakfast at the Sunlight Cafe, a health-food haven in the heart of Seattle. "It's here!" I told Al, my voice catching somewhere between laughter and awe. I stared at that page throughout our entire meal, hardly tasting a thing. I was a published author!

My thoughts returned to the moment when my writing dreams had first taken root. I'd attended a Seattle writers' group as a guest of my teacher, Fern, who had published a book on photography. She'd already inspired me and was now opening up another world with even more possibilities.

It wasn't just any writers' group. To join, you had to be published internationally. That night, New York Times bestselling author J.A. Jance stood up, so tall I thought she was standing on a table, and announced her latest J.P. Beaumont book. She was radiant, confident, and completely in her element. I could feel the sparks of creativity in the air. These were my people, and I wanted to be part of that group.

Over time, more of my writing got published. A story I'd written, called *The Red Plaid Cookbook*, appeared in *The Crone Chronicles*, a glossy quarterly magazine for saging women.

Barnes & Noble stores featured the magazine nationwide for three months, and I wasn't even a crone when I'd written it!

The international publication I'd been working

toward came through Unity Magazine. A psychologist had written an article about the seasons of life, and my poem *Autumn* fit perfectly. It was inset on a page with a beautiful fall scene of a senior man sitting on a park bench.

Autumn

Summer silently slips away
Autumn settles in
Claiming its rightful place
In the everlasting cycle
An in-between kind of season
Lingering in the space
Of what was
And what will be
Summer is our youth
Autumn is letting go
Shedding golden leaves as
We cling to remembrances of days gone by
Of birth and growth
Love and grief
Memories that sustain the soul
On its eternal journey
Harvest time
A time of reflection and gratitude
The wise prepare
For the silver winter ahead.

Becoming an author felt natural. But I wrote with urgency, as if time were a gift of grace, and life could end at any moment.

I seized every experience as if it might slip away, and I'd have to wait another turn of the soul to express myself again.

Only later did I understand why.

~

AFTER TWO YEARS at the Zen-like dental office, I felt an undercurrent of unrest. I longed for the country — the feel of soil underfoot, the stillness of open skies. Then a poem came through about living in the countryside.

My nudge to move lined up with a growing unease in the world at large. Y2K was looming. There were warnings of power grids failing, banks collapsing, and even martial law. Midnight of the year 2000 could bring anything.

We received an invitation. Friends offered us a place to park a trailer on their orchard land out on the Olympic Peninsula. Rows of apple trees, open space. A place to breathe. We arrived a few months before the Y2K countdown, with a home on wheels and two slightly confused cats. With a little faith and a lot of canned goods, we got ready for whatever was coming next.

When the clock struck midnight on New Year's Eve, we did get hit by a bug, but it wasn't the computer bug the world had been worrying about. Instead, we were bitten by the seasonal flu. We both came down with it and spent the night in bed, feverish and miserable.

The computers survived Y2K just fine. We were the ones who crashed.

It didn't take long for our small town to feel like home.

I eased into its gentler rhythm, where people actually talked to one another in stores. The lines were short, even at Costco, and no one seemed to be in a hurry. There were no freeways, only open roads, quiet skies, and friendly faces.

After years in the city, it felt a bit like heaven on earth.

And soon, people were calling me Susan again. More people used that name than ever before—not only when I was writing.

"Hi, Susan!" they called.

They said it as if they remembered me.

And sometimes I wondered if they really did.

16

PERFECTLY OUT OF PLACE

I took a job that turned out to be the polar opposite of the Zen-like clinic I'd left behind.

The office didn't match the town's relaxed vibe. It seemed polished, precise, and a little too perfect. To patients, it looked like a five-star hotel: every detail in place, every orchid in bloom. There was heart there, but it lived under pressure. We cared, yet moved carefully, afraid to miss a step or say the wrong thing.

We started each day with a staff meeting, which I led. I was in the hot seat, questioned and corrected in front of everyone before my coffee even kicked in.

"Sally, next time, please confirm the insurance before calling the lab," the doctor's wife would say, her tone crisp and professional. Everybody knew I'd just screwed up. Unacceptable.

"Of course," I'd reply, making a note and moving on.

It set the tone for the day: efficient and orderly, but missing the warmth and laughter I'd known before.

I wondered why I'd landed there. What was Spirit trying to show me? Perhaps it was the cost of perfection, or how easily joy can slip away when image takes its place. Whatever the reason, I felt the difference.

People stopped calling me Susan, and maybe that was fitting. I wasn't myself. I was playing a part—efficient, polite, professional. At least during working hours. Nothing creative stirred in me at that desk. No poems, no stories. It was all business: teeth and money.

I wrote at night and on weekends, but the office buried all trace of that part of me each morning when I arrived. The creative self that came alive after hours couldn't breathe in that perfect space.

There was little room for personality or independent thought. In retrospect, we were like the Borg on *Star Trek*: a collective hive of ten workers wired for efficiency, expected to think and act as one unit. Still, somewhere beneath the surface, a part of me was waiting, remembering what it felt like to be free.

I stayed in that beautiful pressure cooker for the money. The job paid the bills, and I met patients who later became dear friends.

Looking back, even in that challenging environment, Spirit was still at work, quietly planting seeds I would recognize later.

After a couple of years, things unraveled. It started with a toothache.

One day, a tooth that had been bothering me for weeks began to throb, and I knew it needed to come out. It had all the signs of a fracture—symptoms I was familiar with from my years as an oral surgery tech. I pleaded with the dentist to extract it, but he was hesitant.

"If you don't pull it out, I'll do it myself!" I warned him. He knew I might. Sure enough, the tooth came out in two pieces. It was beyond repair, and I was relieved to be done with it.

We were leaving for Arizona in two days, and I thought I'd be fine to travel.

But life had other plans. An unseen infection from the extraction had already begun its journey to my heart.

17

THE JOB THAT SET ME FREE

The cookie was too sweet; the sun too strong. I pressed a cold Dr. Pepper against my cheek, trying to cool the heat radiating off my skin. It was over a hundred degrees at high noon. No breeze. No shade. I should have stayed in the car, but the cactus garden beckoned.

"Are you sure you want to do this?" my husband said. "Don't stay too long!"

Camera in hand, I followed the dusty path to the garden.

We'd just spent a couple of days visiting friends in Scottsdale, Arizona, and I wasn't quite myself, still healing from oral surgery and running on caffeine and sugar. But I didn't want to miss the trip we had planned. Earlier that day, we'd stopped for a large Dr. Pepper and a pink-frosted cookie—my version of fuel. I pushed through the dry air and relentless sun, trying to soak in the beauty with every shot.

The real trouble started an hour later, when we left the garden. We were heading north toward Las Vegas, a long stretch of highway winding through desert hills with nothing in sight for miles. No towns, no gas stations, not even another car. And no paramedics or hospitals either. If something went wrong, you were on your own. Just sun, sand, and silence.

That's when it hit.

My heart flipped in my chest, or at least, it felt like it. Arrhythmia slammed into me like a hammer. Then everything went black for fifteen seconds. That's all it was. But when you are miles from anywhere, fifteen seconds is an eternity. My breath came out in wisps; my hands were clammy. My heart was misfiring, and I didn't know how to stop it.

When I told my husband, he stayed outwardly calm, focused on the road, but I could feel his worry. We had no choice but to keep going.

We pressed on to Las Vegas, where Al had a music performance scheduled that afternoon at a friend's retirement home. Millie Moore was in her late eighties with a heart condition. I didn't want him to cancel, so I went with him. Millie and I walked arm in arm through the hallway, she dragging her oxygen tank and I with my newly misfiring heart. It was terrifying. The arrhythmia persisted, but Millie comforted me. We were two women with fragile hearts, steadying each other.

That night, we flew home on a red-eye. Somehow, I made it through. The next morning, the hospital fitted me with a heart monitor to wear for a week.

The diagnosis came back: PACs—extra heartbeats that feel like flutters or skipped beats.

Not that uncommon.

But they triggered something else: a panic attack that hit me at work. Right there in the dental office, my heart skipped wildly, and it felt like the walls were closing in on me.

Panic attacks don't go over well in an environment that demands perfection, and the office manager, Beth, confronted me. "If you want to keep working here, you'll need an evaluation from a mental health specialist."

I agreed. Honestly, I hoped it might help. I didn't want another attack. But I wasn't sure whether Beth cared more about the office ambiance or my well-being.

I chose a local psychiatrist. Maybe overkill, but I wanted a seasoned professional. His gray hair and wall of diplomas suggested he was close to retirement. Kind eyes and a gentle voice helped me relax. "What can I do for you, Sally?"

I told him about the arrhythmia, the panic, the blinding moments in the desert. He listened carefully and taught me some simple breathing techniques.

"Most arrhythmias aren't dangerous," he said.

It was the first time I really exhaled since I'd left the desert.

Our conversation took a turn when I brought up the faith I was raised in, and he mentioned he was a Mormon elder.

Of course he was. There was something familiar about him: his mannerisms and speech. Mormonism had been the faith of my birth, ingrained in me from childhood, even though I'd long since stepped away. Still, it lingered in the corners, like a script I hadn't fully erased.

He talked about the LDS perspective on the soul and pre-existence. I nodded and said, "Maybe." Then I told him something I rarely shared. Strangers had been calling me Susan for years, and I believed it was a past-life memory. He smiled kindly, and I knew we'd just agreed to disagree.

Before I left, he said, "You think deeply. Most people don't. That's a gift."

After that visit, whatever residue of Mormon doctrine had persisted in my mind was gone.

~

When the front office was downsized, I was the one who got laid off, and they gave me a lovely going-away party. I smiled graciously while silently rejoicing. *Thank God I was done with that place.*

That afternoon I drove home feeling unexpectedly light—not just better, but free.

I had just walked in the door when an urgent need to write came over me. I grabbed some paper.

The verses were unlike anything I'd written before. They told the story of a caterpillar who dreamed of becoming a butterfly.

I leaned back and looked at the page, unsure what to make of them.

"What in the world is this?" I said to myself. "And where did it come from?"

Then I heard it.

A strong male voice. Gentle but unmistakably clear. I'd heard it before, years earlier, when I was a young mother in need of guidance.

The voice answered my question: "*This is a children's book that will go around the world in five years.*"

And it did. Almost to the day.

18

"IF IT BREAKS, CAN YOU FIX IT?"

It's not every day you get laid off and assigned a new life purpose by a spirit guide.

I sat there, oddly at peace. The message was clear: the poem would become a children's book.

Wow. I had some work to do first.

Back then, *The Writer's Market* was the go-to resource, a hefty paperback filled with publisher listings. I flipped to the children's book section, made a list, wrote query letters, and tucked my manuscript into large manila envelopes. One by one, I mailed them to publishers across the country.

Rejection letters came back. When you get a letter from a publisher, especially one like Simon & Schuster, it's exciting. I saved every letter and set the project aside for the time being.

A month later, I took a job as office manager for Dr. Grant, an orthodontist. On my first day, the gal I was replacing was showing me the ropes. Unfortunately, she had just taken a sip of coffee when I cracked a joke. She tried to hold back a laugh but couldn't, and the next thing I knew, she sprayed her drink all over the front of my new white sweater.

I glanced down in horror.

"I'm so sorry!" she said through tears of laughter.

I knew this was going to be a good job.

Dr. Grant was kind, funny, and brilliant. I worked with him for ten years. He trusted me completely. He had even known my uncle back in dental school.

"I really liked your uncle," Dr. Grant said. "I remember him well. He was a pharmacist before he went into dentistry."

That made me feel like I belonged. Dr. Grant and I shared a connection from the very beginning through my Uncle Bob.

Most of our patients were kids, ages five through nineteen, though we had adults too. I worked solo at the front desk, greeting everyone who came and went. Parents and kids often stopped to chat, and that was fine by me. I had never worked in such a comfortable office, and it was only a short time before I felt right at home.

The building itself was unusual for an orthodontic office. Dr. Grant designed and built it in the 1970s, complete with a swimming pool and workout room. My desk faced floor-to-ceiling windows, one offering a view of the Olympic Mountains, the other of the Strait of Juan de Fuca. Not a bad setup.

THAT SUMMER, while I settled into my new job, life outside the office was moving in a very different direction.

I made the drive back and forth to Edmonds often to visit my parents. My dad was in the hospital, still able to speak but drifting in and out of consciousness. He had lived with leukemia for eleven years, nearly three years longer than doctors expected for that type. He once told me he wanted to live until seventy-five.

Two months after his seventy-fifth birthday, doctors moved him to the ICU. A breathing tube kept him alive as he lay still and silent.

My mom never gave up hope.

For fifty years, my parents had done everything together: raised a family of five kids, and in their later years, traveled to Dixieland jazz festivals. Even during my dad's chemo treatments, when he found the strength, they danced in the living room as if nothing had changed. Music had always filled the house. The neighbors could attest to that!

One hot August morning, I stood with my mom in the kitchen while she finished processing berries from the backyard. My dad had been in the ICU for three weeks, with no change. Yet my mother's focus was steady, almost ritualistic. I was puzzled, as if something didn't fit. Deep down I knew he was passing soon, yet watching my mom said it wasn't so.

Hope

I watched my mother
carefully washing the fresh blueberries.
"These are for your dad," she said.

Rinsing, sorting, and freezing berries
as he lay in intensive care,
machines and medicine keeping him alive
for another day.

I said nothing,
just nodded and thought,
Yes, Dad loves these.

I had to get back to work, at least for a couple of days. My thoughts kept returning to my dad and how far away my family was. I couldn't concentrate well.

At my desk, I'd just started working on a stack of insurance claims when I felt the strangest sensation, like a feather being pulled from deep inside me, rising slowly and slipping out through my chest.

I froze.

A moment later, both phone lines rang.

My brother was on one line, my sister on the other.

They both said, "Dad is gone."

When I'd kissed him goodbye two days earlier, I felt it might be the last time. The nurse had warned us that once they removed the breathing tube, he wouldn't last long. I worried that if I stayed for the passing, I might not handle it well, because I'd never seen anyone die before. My dad and I were so close, I couldn't imagine watching him take his last breath.

Seeing his head resting on a hospital pillow, hooked up to machines, was almost more than I could bear.

He spoke to me one last time after they removed the tube. He struggled for breath, frowned, and said, "Sally, if it breaks, can you fix it?"

I didn't know exactly what he meant, but I nodded.

"Yes, I can fix it, Dad."

It was such an odd question, especially at that moment.

But in time, I understood.

19

JUST ASK

Some days you don't want to remember. But you do, because even those days hold something sacred.

After the phone calls from my brother and sister, I grabbed my purse and told the staff and doctor my dad had passed away and I needed to leave immediately.

"Go, Sally. May God go with you," Dr. Grant said.

I'll always remember his words and the look on his face. In that moment, I felt deeply blessed to be surrounded by such kindness.

I set out for the three-hour drive to my parents' home and turned up the radio to drown out my raw emotions. When I arrived in their driveway, I stayed in the car for a few minutes, avoiding the front door. I left the music blaring, then turned off the engine and stepped onto the cement steps of my childhood home.

After the hugs, I sank onto the sofa. It was August, but the air felt wintry. Grief had cooled the room.

I looked into everyone's faces and saw the trauma they'd been through at the hospital. Though I had escaped that part, I was still affected. I knew the exact moment his soul left, even from miles away.

The living room was full of family, yet it felt hollow. Dad's chair sat empty. We all kept looking at it.

In the days that followed, we took care of funeral business, and I busied myself making a poster covered in family photos. Across the top, in sparkling gold letters, I wrote *What a Wonderful Life*, because we all knew Dad's favorite song was *What a Wonderful World*, sung by Louis Armstrong.

The morning of the funeral came too quickly. We were all trying to keep things light. I joked, "Sorry I didn't wash my white Honda Civic. It's pretty dusty. At least I'm not leading the funeral procession." Surely Mom would choose a nicer car to ride in.

But at the last minute, she rode with me.

I cringed as she climbed into my car. I worried it wasn't dignified enough for the occasion. But my mom never hesitated, and I realized it didn't matter as long as we were together, mother and eldest daughter.

I turned the key in the ignition, and we both jumped.

The radio was still blasting music.

Then we heard the song.

Louis Armstrong was singing *What a Wonderful World.*

We looked at each other and smiled. He was with us. All was well.

After the church service, Mom jumped right back into my car, and I led the procession after all.

~

LIFE CONTINUED, but I moved through it on autopilot. I missed my dad's voice. His last words echoed in my mind again and again: "*If it breaks, can you fix it?*"

I'd always been by his side when he fixed things. I tagged along with him to the hardware store and learned about household repair. I kept him company when he was repairing his car or working in the garden. And later, when I had a house of my own, he was always a phone call away, guiding me from afar.

It took me a while to figure out what his last words meant. Little things began to happen, and I noticed he was still guiding me.

A few days after the funeral, we needed to access some important documents that were in my father's safe. But no one could crack the combination. My mom had already tried, and so had my brothers and sisters. Still, I went downstairs to attempt it.

I opened the study door, and the faint, musty scent of old paperwork met me like an embrace from the past. His old real estate sign, *Seattle Homes*, leaned against the wall. I sat in the silence and let my grief settle. Then I placed my hands on the safe's dial.

I'd never opened it before. No one had, except him.

Show me, Dad.

I glanced at the faded numbers on the scrap of paper no one had been able to decipher and listened as if my dad were instructing me. My fingers moved with a confidence that wasn't mine.

Click. It opened!

That was when I understood his last words.

It wasn't a riddle after all. It was a reminder: If something breaks, ask for help, just like I always had. And if I reached out, he'd be there.

My dad's death opened a new door to the spirit world. In his physical absence, my perception shifted. I found I could easily tune into a heavenly realm of different vibrations, carried on waves of pulsing light and love. When I thought of my father, I felt closer to that dimension than ever before.

As a ham radio operator, I was familiar with the art of fine-tuning a dial and listening for a steady signal through the static. I rode those waves the same way, receiving impressions that felt more like frequencies than words.

My dad had spent years listening for signals of his own on a 1947 Crosley tabletop radio, its ivory Bakelite cabinet yellowed with age. It once sat in his downstairs shop, pulling voices and music out of the air while he worked.

After he passed on, it was the one possession of his I wanted to take home. I put the vintage radio on my kitchen counter, between a wicker basket and an aloe plant.

To my surprise, I discovered it served a purpose far greater than broadcasting news and music: it somehow connected me to him. What we call "the other side" no longer felt distant or unreachable. The Crosley reminded me that the space between souls is never as far as we think.

20

A REUNION ACROSS LIFETIMES

For ten years, the name Susan followed me, spoken by strangers and friends alike.

Who *was* Susan?

One day, home from work with a slight cold, I decided it was time to find out. So I closed my eyes and begged God to give me an answer. While I waited for God's reply, I did something I rarely could during my busy work week—I turned on daytime television.

There on the screen was Montel Williams interviewing Sylvia Browne, the renowned medium. As if by divine arrangement, she was discussing her new book, *Life on the Other Side.*

Her presence drew me in, and I listened, captivated, as she spoke about past lives. Without hesitation, I threw on my clothes and headed downtown to find her book.

Would it hold the key to the mystery of Susan?

Once I got my hands on the book, I couldn't put it down. It was as if I stood in a doorway between worlds.

TWO DAYS LATER, still in that altered state, I showed up for a worship service. The topic of the day was "past lives."

Since I strongly suspected that the name Susan was connected to a past life, I told my Susan story to the group, and then blurted, "I'm ready for some answers." That moment set an amazing sequence of events in motion...

The next day, I returned to work, and on my lunch break, my car seemed to have a mind of its own. It took me to Gottschalk's Department Store.

I sat in the parking lot, took a few bites of a tuna sandwich, then went inside, where a red sweater called to me. I picked it up and headed toward the checkout counter, but was stopped short.

A striking Japanese woman approached me.

"Here, come here. I'll take care of you," she said. She seemed a little older than me and moved with the elegance of a dancer. Her shoulder-length black hair fell in soft waves, every strand in place. In her silk floral blouse and gold jewelry, she looked dressed for a night on the town, not like someone working under the fluorescent lights of a department store.

Her nametag said "Aiko."

She gently grabbed my arm and guided me across the store to her counter in the perfume department, where the two of us were alone. Salespeople don't normally take your arm and lead you somewhere. I wasn't sure whether it was the novelty of that or something else, but I felt slightly off-balance as I opened my purse to get my wallet.

I handed her my Visa card.

She stared at it, looked up at me, then back at the card. "Oh my God, you're not Sally, you're Susan!"

She paused and locked eyes with me, repeating the name I'd been called for ten years.

"Susan... oh my God, I just got chills."

I was so stunned that all I could do was nod. *Yes, that's who I am.*

I met Aiko's gaze in awe, as if I'd just been handed the missing piece of the most important puzzle of my life. It felt like waking from amnesia.

She said, "I knew you a long time ago." Then she explained that when she was five, she had drowned and been brought back to life, awakening the gift of second sight.

She added, "I don't know who this Sally is. I just know Susan."

She wrapped her arms around me and pulled me close. Silent tears streamed down my face.

As we embraced, years—perhaps lifetimes—flashed across the screen of my mind like an old silent movie.

Anguish pierced me as I witnessed a scene of war and tragedy.

Then the images softened and shifted to another time, somewhere gentle and familiar, filled with beauty and grace. Suddenly I remembered Aiko.

Her features and speech were completely different in this life, so they had thrown me off. But the embrace connected our souls, and in that instant, I saw my beloved friend again.

It was almost too much to take in. Three or four lifetimes condensed into ten seconds, ending in the joy of reunion and deep gratitude for an answered prayer. I was overloaded, nearly speechless, and I needed to ground myself quickly. So I said what wise people throughout history have no doubt said when they experience a monumental spiritual event: "I need to go eat my tuna sandwich now."

21

WHEN TWO LIFETIMES MET

The line between past and present was fading, and memories long asleep were stirring.

But before I visited Aiko again, I wanted to see how much I could discover on my own. On the way to the beach, my favorite place for clarity and rejuvenation, I told Al I wanted to know more about Susan.

Al was driving, so I took advantage of the moment to close my eyes and ask Spirit.

I need to know about Susan. Please show me.

I got an immediate impression that I had written children's poetry during Susan's life. But a sadness tinged that memory, and I didn't know why.

Then came a vision of a grassy field overlooking a vast blue ocean, a place that felt strangely familiar.

A FEW WEEKS LATER, it was time to see Aiko. I walked into the store and there she was—my friend from another era—standing by the perfume counter as if she had been waiting for me. We embraced and chatted easily about the weather and our health.

Then I asked her if she knew anything more about Susan, and, amazingly, she said, "It was a long time ago —England, late 1800s. You were very young, beautiful, and sweet. You wrote children's poetry. And oh, Susan loved flowers very much. You lived near the ocean and we would often walk the beach, where you would say, 'Isn't this beautiful?' My name was Isabel."

I stood there as two lifetimes melted into one and said, "I write children's stories now, and I'm a flower photographer."

Once again, I walked away, my feet barely touching the ground. My circuits were full. Aiko had just confirmed my intuitive insights!

The floodgates opened wide. I could suddenly sense visions of England, other friends, and writing. As I immersed myself in these new feelings, something bothered me. I needed more information.

Aiko had said I'd been young and beautiful in that past life. Young. So when and how had I died? I phoned her and asked. She seemed disturbed by the question, but said, "High fever."

"Influenza?" I asked.

"Yes. Thirty-two years old, only," she said in her Japanese-English way.

"Thank you, that explains a lot," I said. As a photographer in this lifetime, I'd been drawn to headstones that read *Died of influenza*. They had always fascinated me. It also explained my lifelong germ phobia and the strange feeling that I would never see forty in this lifetime, an age I have now passed.

Shortly after my conversation with Aiko, my husband and I took a trip to Victoria, B.C., where the Royal B.C. Museum was exhibiting a bedroom from the 1800s. Suddenly, I saw a vision of my former Susan self on her deathbed when I'd said to God, "Why now? I'm not done yet."

Writing for children and surrounded by kindred souls, had been a peaceful, unhurried life. But it ended with unpublished stories and unfinished dreams.

It was like riding a beautiful carousel horse, one hoof raised in motion. And just as the music began, the ride was over.

~

AT THE NEXT WORSHIP SERVICE, a month later, I told everyone, "Guess what? Here's the rest of the Susan story!"

Jo, a close friend of only a few months, smiled slyly as I spoke. When I finished, she held out her hand and said, "Hi, Susan. I'm J.R. Caldwell, a writer from England in the late 1800s. My friends called me Becky."

Jo—"Becky"—continued, "Since I met you, I've felt

like I could trust you with anything. That's very unusual for me, since I normally keep to myself about personal matters."

We hugged, and once again, tears of warm remembrance slid down my face.

22

THE DAY NORMAL DISAPPEARED

My days at the orthodontic office went on as usual.

Dr. Grant talked as much as he worked, and he managed to do both at full speed. He'd lean against my desk between patients, chatting away, and despite it all, I got my work done.

The oldies station played in the background, and the steady stream of children brought life and laughter to my day.

Our satellite office in Port Townsend drew a different crowd: organic, New Age, and New Thought.

Even though Dr. Grant was a conservative Christian, he welcomed everyone with genuine appreciation. Our practice reached people from every corner of the peninsula.

He especially loved Mexico and its people, and our Hispanic patients loved him for it.

"¡Mira esa sonrisa, perfecto!"

(Look at that smile—perfect!)

The kids would flash him their best grins, displaying a mouthful of metal and colorful rubber bands.

I'll never forget the kindness of the people we served. The tribal families brought us gifts of fresh halibut, salmon, or handmade crafts as their way of saying thank you. And a Hispanic family once surprised us with tamales for the entire staff, still warm and wrapped in corn husks.

Each day was so entertaining I started calling our office *The Dr. Grant Show*. Everyone who walked through the door became part of the cast. Surrounded by the energy of the kids, I felt ageless.

I didn't realize it then, but my part in the show was about to take an abrupt intermission.

I'd been working at Dr. Grant's for two years when Christmas rolled around again. Toothbrushes hung from the office tree, and Bing Crosby crooned *White Christmas*.

It was the second holiday season without my dad, and I thought about going back home to Edmonds. Just picturing his empty armchair left a hollow feeling in my chest. As the oldest daughter of five children, I needed to be there for my mom.

But just as the holiday approached, I started feeling "off." A strange stomachache accompanied by bone-deep exhaustion.

"I can't make it over, Mom. I don't feel good," I told her.

"Do you have a fever?" she asked.

"No, just exhausted."

"Well, come on over. You can relax on the couch. We need you here!"

Christmas morning arrived, and I still felt sick. I called my mom again to decline the invitation.

"Sally, just get in your car and drive! It's Christmas!"

Against my better judgment, I did.

Only a few cars were lined up at the ferry terminal, not the usual holiday crowd. I got out to walk to the restroom, and suddenly felt a strange popping sensation in my head, followed by a wave of nausea. My left leg weakened, and I had to lean on Al just to walk.

I thought I was over the worst of it, but I wasn't. The next day, a wave of fire shot up my spine, followed by more numbness and tingling in my arms and legs. More neurological episodes arrived. Once, when I was alone in the house, I couldn't lift my left arm for several seconds. I breathed a sigh of gratitude when it moved again.

Doctors couldn't pinpoint the cause. I even had tests for mercury and heavy metal poisoning, since I'd handled mercury in my early years in dentistry. Were those years coming to haunt me now?

My brain MRIs showed several concerning spots. They suspected multiple sclerosis or possibly stroke activity, so while I waited for answers, I turned to an old friend: poetry.

Writing helped me process the unknown. It gave shape to my mystery illness. The one thing I knew was that my definition of normal had left abruptly on Christmas Day. I'd stepped off the train in the deserted town of Nowhere, alone, without a compass or map, unsure of what was around the corner. My doctor said only time would tell if I had MS.

Suddenly

It was Christmas Day
When Normal went away
I stood alone
Watching in horror
As a heavy steel door
Appeared without warning
Slamming shut
My world, my birthright.

Now, occasionally
A bit of fresh wind blows in
From around the cracks
And sweet muffled sounds
Of life tease my ears
Reminding me of before.

How foolishly I assumed

Life to be a deep well
Of health, vitality, and choice
Blessings taken for granted no more.

Everything familiar was gone: work, routine, even the feeling of being myself.

I didn't know if I would heal or what healing might look like. But I knew nothing happens by chance, that even illness is a language of the soul. As my world slowed to stillness, I listened.

In that silence, more poetry arrived, slowly at first, then more insistently.

Healing sometimes begins not in the body, but in words that come from the heart.

23

ONE SMALL MIRACLE AT A TIME

Like my favorite poet, Emily Dickinson, I lived behind a windowpane, waiting for poetry to find me. During those months, I felt suspended between participation and observation.

It was a good thing I had the desire to write, because writing was what I held onto when the doctors couldn't help.

Fear came and went in waves. Would I have another scary episode like that day at the ferry dock, the wind whipping across the water, the ferry horn sounding far away? I replayed that scene often, as if reliving it might change the ending.

All I wanted was to get back to that wild and crazy Dr. Grant Show. But instead I was at home, watching the days go by. I wondered if inspiration had come to Emily the same way it was coming to me—through solitude and stillness.

The best part of my day was actually the night, because my dreams were rich with adventure. I met people and did things in the dream state I couldn't do while awake. And when an enthusiastic morning bird pulled me back to earth, I had to admit I was a little cranky.

Morning Bird

I was basking in the slumber
Of night's repose
When morning bird appeared
And threatened to impose
In the shadows of a dream
His singing beckoned me
Calling me to earth
When I longed to be free

To explore and create
Beyond all space and time
In kaleidoscopic worlds
Limitless, sublime

Cease your revelry, I begged
I must prolong this night
For dawn will soon arrive
To end my dreamtime flight

For a time, I lingered
In the place where worlds combine
Which was true reality?
Both earth and dreams were mine

Then gently I returned
With the rising sun
As morning bird proclaimed
A new day had begun!

BACK THEN, I didn't know the birds singing outside my window were chickadees, sparrows, and four different kinds of finches. It would be years until I became a bird photographer—out there with camera in hand, turning moments like that into award-winning photographs. For now, I simply waited. Watching, healing, and writing. It was all I could do, and it had to be enough.

Six months passed before I could return to work, and even then, only part-time. My coworker was the dentist's sweet wife, Marilyn. Before my illness, she had mostly stayed behind the scenes as the bookkeeper, writing our checks.

Marilyn had taken over all my duties when I left, and now she graciously welcomed me back, adjusting to my needs with kindness, understanding that my health was still fragile.

No one could put a name on my condition, so it remained a mystery for years. But to the Grants, it didn't matter what the label was. They never treated me like a problem to be solved.

"Sally, you're back!" I heard it again and again as kids and parents came through the door of the happiest orthodontic office around.

I wasn't entirely back, not yet. But I had returned to the place where my laughter had once lived. It didn't matter that my paycheck was smaller. I was alive, and my shorter hours were enough to feed my spirit. I was deeply grateful for this second chance.

I took a renewed interest in our patients, especially the bright little souls who came bouncing through the door. It was as if they could feel the love in that space.

ONE DAY, I got an envelope in the mail. It changed my life.

Right before I got sick, I'd felt a nudge to resubmit *The Caterpillar's Dream* manuscript. But first, I had to name the caterpillar. In a flash, it came to me: Kip.

I rewrote the book to include his name, then turned once again to the *Writer's Market*, selecting twenty-five publishers and mailing fresh copies of the manuscript. Over the following months, the familiar pattern returned—rejection letters, twenty-four of them, one after another. I let it go. *Oh well.* I didn't know what else I could have done differently.

There was only one publisher I hadn't heard from.

One day, Al walked through the front door grinning, holding a thick brown envelope. "I have a feeling this isn't a rejection letter!" he said.

I opened it carefully. My eyes went wide.

It was a book contract with my name on it. The title read *Intention to Print* from Journey Stone Creations, a small Christian children's book publisher in Ohio. I took a deep breath and let it sink in. They would have it ready within a year. *The Caterpillar's Dream* was going to be born, and Kip would touch children's hearts all over the world.

"I have one year to get strong enough to do book signings," I told Al, trusting that this gift had come in divine timing and that my healing would rise to meet it.

The woman who had once watched life through a window was stepping back into the world. Even on the hard days, I held on to the certainty that something greater was guiding me, one small miracle at a time.

24

THE PROMISE UNFOLDS

The book publishing world is full of moving parts, but the most important ones are people.

The year-long publishing process began with illustrator Randy Monces. I never spoke to him directly. Once the publisher took over, I became more of an observer, watching from the sidelines and hoping the artist understood my vision.

The first black-and-white sketch I saw was of Kip. Adorable and full of charm, his open, friendly expression captured my heart. It was love at first sight. Every few days, more sketches appeared. Somehow, without a single word between us, Randy had brought my verses to life with images more enchanting than I had ever imagined.

In my mind, I'd seen Kip's world with lush forests, sunlight filtering through tropical leaves, and a sense of wonder on every page. Randy lived in the Philippines, surrounded by the very beauty I had envisioned, and that's exactly what he drew.

Then came the color. The black-and-white sketches blossomed into a living world, vibrant and full of life.

The Caterpillar's Dream would join a series of books called *Little Nuggets.* These were short, ninety-second stories for children two to six years old, with bright covers and bindings reminiscent of the *Little Golden Books* we all loved as kids. I couldn't wait to hold my copy and see it nestled among the others in the series.

I felt a kinship with everyone at Journey Stone Creations and with their mission of creating wholesome, values-based books for children and families. Their titles, from the *Angels With Attitudes* series to *Stranger Danger*, all shared one purpose: to offer uplifting, age-appropriate stories parents and teachers could trust.

One day a special package arrived. Al handed it to me, like he'd done the previous year with the book contract. I carefully tore it open and pulled out the little book with Kip the caterpillar on the cover. My eyes were moist. It was the birth of more than a book, and I remembered the words I'd heard years before:

"It will be a children's book in five years." That assurance from Spirit came full circle, and with it came another gift. The part of me known as Susan, who had carried the sorrow of dying before her work was published, was at last fulfilled. Through me, she now held the joyful little caterpillar book in her hands.

Booksellers across the U.S. received *The Little Nuggets* series. And then, cases of *The Caterpillar's Dream* arrived on my doorstep for local book signings, and I was ready!

It was perfect timing. My neighbor, Lani, had just opened Adventures in Learning, a bookstore for home-schooling, and was eager to host my book-release event.

We had fun setting it up. I brought platters of fruit and cookies and armfuls of shiny green, blue, and yellow balloons to match the colors of my book. I'd called a reporter in advance to cover the event and get the word out—there was a new caterpillar in town!

I sat at my book-signing table next to a stack of unsigned books and took it all in. This was the moment Susan had waited for. But I wasn't thinking about the past. I was living in the moment, just as the children were. I watched kids and parents pick books from the display the publisher had sent, a five-foot-tall red cardboard stand filled with rows of *Little Nuggets*.

Laughter and chatter filled the air, and everywhere I looked, someone was holding *The Caterpillar's Dream.*

Pen in hand, I came up with a signature that I still use today—"Happy Dreams!" As I signed the first copy, a reporter from the local news snapped a photo. I've kept the newspaper article as a reminder of that unforgettable day.

And that day was just the beginning.

At work, Dr. Grant said, "Sally, why don't you set up something to sell and sign your books? You could put them right here!" He pointed to the reception desk, the perfect spot where everyone would see them.

"That would be fun!" I said. "Thank you!"

Everything we did centered on kids. What were the chances that I'd be working for an orthodontist who not only supported my little book, but invited me to display, sell, and sign it right at the front desk?

As time went on, I witnessed the impact it had on the kids. They realized they could create something too: that writing a book or a story wasn't out of reach. The kids often lingered at my desk instead of heading straight to the waiting room because they were eager to talk about school, sports, or whatever they loved doing.

Relationships lasted long after the braces came off. Even now, over fifteen years later, I still run into some of those kids—now grown—and they stop to talk as if no time has passed. Every so often, one of them tells me they still have the copy of *The Caterpillar's Dream* that I signed just for them.

And that's why it mattered: a child could see how something imagined in the heart could become real in the world.

25

KIP IN THE SPOTLIGHT

The Voice I'd heard had big ambitions for my little caterpillar. It said *The Caterpillar's Dream* would circle the globe. For a small Ohio-based publisher, that was a tall order, so I tucked the promise away and enjoyed the sweet hum of local enthusiasm.

Back then, being a children's author drew attention. That was before self-publishing became popular. Self-published books were often brushed off as "vanity" projects. But kids didn't care about any of that, and honestly, neither did I. I was simply grateful to be working with a publisher who had real integrity and vision.

Doors opened for me.

"Would you come read your book to my class?" a teacher asked over the phone. "The kids would love to meet a real author."

A real author. I glanced around the kitchen as if that was someone else.

Soon I was visiting elementary school classrooms, reading aloud and answering questions. I was even asked to judge a school-wide writing contest.

"We'd be honored if you'd choose the winners," the principal said.

Looking back, it still amazes me. I didn't have a teaching credential or a literary degree, just my dental background and a heart full of stories.

In 2007, the publishing world was very different. Authors had no social media for promotion. So reaching readers was slow and personal: book signings, printed newsletters, bookstore tables, and chance meetings. Getting *The Caterpillar's Dream* noticed on a wide scale in that climate was nearly impossible.

Here's how it unfolded:

Just a year after the book's release, a remarkable man named Mark Smith helped fulfill the prophecy to bring *The Caterpillar's Dream* to the world.

Mark was a warm, easy-going, creative entrepreneur with a salt-and-pepper beard and a quick smile. I liked him right away. "I'm going to take good care of Kip, Sally," he said. "This is going to be fun, and I want you to be part of everything we do!"

Mark then introduced what was at the time a new technology: digital children's books read in a gentle voice, set to soft music, with pages that turned on their own. Teachers, including Smith's wife Lois, narrated the stories.

The Smiths named the digital storybooks Maggie Tales™, after their four-year-old Havanese dog.

The Caterpillar's Dream was the very first book developed in this new format. They were portable stories that could play on almost anything back then, from iPods to handheld gaming devices.

"These stories were made for real life," Mark explained. "For moments when a child needs something engaging. Waiting in line. Restaurants. Long car rides."

With his background in consumer products, technology, and marketing, Mark took Maggie Tales™ to the New York International Toy Fair, where each year people launch and discover new toys and children's products.

"They're going to love Kip," he told me. And they did.

BusinessWeek TV featured Kip the caterpillar and Maggie Tales™ as a "2008 Hot New Product" on nationwide television. I watched Kip on TV like a proud mom.

A couple of weeks later, Mark asked if I'd join him for a future TV appearance.

"We'd be a great promotional team," he said. "You and me together — it would be perfect."

I smiled. "I'm terribly camera shy," I told him.

It was easier than explaining that my stamina came and went without warning.

But some doors open only once. For me, that was one of them, and turning it down remains a lingering regret.

Meanwhile, the digital world was racing ahead. In July 2008, Apple launched the App Store as part of iTunes, offering about 500 apps on opening day. It was the beginning of mobile apps as we know them.

Mark saw the opportunity. He expanded Maggie Tales™ and created the iKidsPlay™ apps with full interactivity: coloring, painting, narration, and creative play designed specifically for young children. Apple released *The Caterpillar's Dream* app for iTunes on November 11, 2008, among the first wave of children's picture-book apps.

Soon after the launch, Mark told me that without a single dollar spent in marketing, *The Caterpillar's Dream* app had been purchased in 18 countries in just the first two weeks.

With his usual humor, he added, "I'm hoping it becomes a cult item in some foreign country and they buy 100,000 copies of the app and the book. Keep your fingers crossed and tell Kip to cross his wings!"

Then came a moment I could never have imagined.

In the summer of 2009, Apple launched its first worldwide app campaign and chose a small group of its favorite standout apps to spotlight in stores around the globe.

At the time, all I knew was that *The Caterpillar's Dream* had been selected from about 400 children's apps, which felt extraordinary on its own. I didn't learn until later that Apple had over 65,000 apps on iTunes that summer, available in 77 countries, so Kip had been selected from less than one percent of all the apps on the platform. Even now, it amazes me. My little caterpillar had stepped into an exclusive circle.

I WAS fifty-five years old when all of that happened.

My mom and I visited an Apple Store to celebrate Kip's big moment. When we entered, we noticed that *The Caterpillar's Dream* was everywhere.

A huge wall mural showed apps streaming out of an iPhone, and there, in the middle of all the new releases was Kip with his little green head and the curl of fur on his crown. When I saw his smiling face, he was no longer just ink and watercolor on paper. He was part of something bigger—innovative and far-reaching.

They also featured Kip in the front window display and included him in a store-wide ceiling mobile.

Over 240 Apple Stores around the world took part in the campaign that summer, and Kip found his way into all of them. When the campaign ended, Al made the trip to Seattle to bring home one of the hanging icons. I still have it, and every once in awhile I gently pluck it out of a white plastic bag with the Apple logo on it. Kip smiles back at me, and I revisit that special day when my mom and I witnessed the miracle of a dream fulfilled.

26

HAPPY DREAMS

The moment you stepped inside Dr. Grant's orthodontic office, you knew it was unlike any other. Bright yellow and cobalt-blue stripes marched across the walls. At times, it felt more like a circus than a clinic. The entire office was designed for kids, and apparently for old souls, too. We all crossed paths under the big top.

One day, fourteen-year-old Laura bounced into the office with a wide grin, leaned on my desk, and said, "Hi, Susie!"

I laughed. "You called me Susie."

"I know, Sally. I wanted to call you *Susan*, but I chose Susie instead."

Laura had been a patient for two years, and I looked forward to her visits. I knew some children recalled previous lives, and I wondered if I was witnessing that now. Had she known me from another time? I began to look at her a little differently, trying to remember something from long ago. I'd smile and ask about her day, but what I really wanted to know was why she'd called me Susie.

Dr. Grant's was a place where kindred souls seemed to meet.

Our ortho assistant had a little boy who fascinated me from the moment I'd met him. He was riding in his mother's Walmart cart, dressed in a tweed suit—jacket, trousers, button-down shirt, tie—topped with a tiny bowler hat. At four years old, he met my eyes with the confidence of someone far older.

His mom leaned closer and said, "Nathan insists on dressing like this every day. He talks about flying planes before he came here and describes the countries he flew over and the aircraft in remarkable detail. I'm convinced he was a World War II pilot, and he dresses the way men once did in England."

His family was Catholic, and they easily could have dismissed it. Instead, they honored the memory he carried into this life and allowed Nathan to be who he was.

Years later, I came across a photo of Nathan on social media. At twenty-one, he stood beside a blue single-engine plane at the local airport. He had earned his pilot's license at twenty and looked completely at home beside that small plane. His love of flying had followed him into this lifetime, now without the shadow of war.

Stories like Nathan's reminded me why I loved writing for children.

Being an author brought its own kind of magic, and I wanted more of it. *The Caterpillar's Dream* had arrived unintentionally, just as my first poem, *Another Springtime*, had. I wondered if I could write another book, this time on purpose, instead of waiting for inspiration to sneak up on me when I wasn't looking.

National book tours were still a thing back then, and I couldn't help picturing myself on one. But my body had its own ideas. Just as I began to feel a little momentum returning, I found myself back at home with a few weeks of forced rest. I felt like a butterfly sent back into the cocoon.

Fortunately, I had a rich dream life. My dreams gave me the adventures I couldn't have while lying weak and isolated in bed. In that quiet space, I asked myself what I could do. It turned out to be the perfect time to write.

I thought dreams might be a subject for a book. Many children hesitate to go to bed, afraid of nightmares, something that often happens when they're trying to process the thoughts and emotions of their day.

What if a child could look forward to dreams? That idea inspired *Rainbow Nights*.

I wanted children to know they are never alone, that love is always near, and they could turn dreams into a nightly adventure.

As I began to write, the lines rhymed in a natural

way, much like when I wrote *The Caterpillar's Dream*. This time, though, the process felt more conscious, with me at the helm, listening to my heart and mind as the words came forth.

I became the child in the story, exploring and experiencing my heart's desire with such joy that I smiled the whole time I wrote.

The finished manuscript was a bedtime story of adventure, curiosity, and fun—proof that even cocoon time had a purpose. When I read it now, a few lines still make me smile:

> Dreamland can be kind of busy,
> with everything in a tizzy!
> Swirling colors and flashing lights,
> tuba music and rainbow nights.
> A little odd, but that's okay.
> Dreams were made to be that way.
> Things look kind of different there,
> you could be wearing purple hair!

My publisher loved the manuscript and planned to publish it the coming year. In the meantime, I had an idea for a third children's book about how color and art can change your mood.

The inspiration came while my husband was creating an online course on the power of color. Arlene Arnold, "The Color Lady" of Transformational Tools™, spent several afternoons at our house recording the course with Al. I listened from the sidelines, fascinated by their conversation, and the urge to write took root.

While they worked on the course, I curled up by the woodstove in our living room and created *Color Me Happy!*

I pictured the illustrations as I wrote each verse and resolved to work directly with an illustrator. I named the main character Sadie after my four-year-old niece. Sadie painted every day and proudly wore the colors on her hands—purples, pinks, yellows, and greens, like a tiny paint palette. She'd smile, display her fingers, and say, "Look, Aunt Sally!"

Journey Stone Creations wanted to publish *Color Me Happy!* right after *Rainbow Nights.* Things were going great. *The Caterpillar's Dream* was thriving, and the new app was taking off beautifully.

What I didn't know was that big changes were brewing in the publishing world. Changes that would affect the future of all three of my books.

27

A NEW DIRECTION

"Let yourself be silently drawn by the strange pull of what you really love. It will not lead you astray." —Rumi

I received unexpected news. My publisher could not publish my next two books. Even more shocking, once the inventory of *The Caterpillar's Dream* ran out, they wouldn't be reprinting it.

But it had nothing to do with my book.

The entire small publishing world was collapsing. Warehouses were full of unsold books, distributors were going bankrupt, and the industry was turning upside down.

By 2008, bookstores were closing, Amazon was changing the way people bought books, and the rise of e-books shook the ground beneath every small press.

Many simply couldn't survive the financial storm. My publisher was one of them, and I recognized what a gift it had been to get published in the short period before everything changed.

The miracles that carried *The Caterpillar's Dream* around the world could not have happened even a year later.

What I did next with that gift was up to me. Even the iTunes app vanished, lost to a behind-the-scenes financial complication between Apple Computer and Mark Smith.

I wasn't really back to where I started. I still owned my book.

"I will not let Kip disappear," I told Patricia, my now-former publisher. If the next step was self-publishing, then I would learn how to do just that. She gave me the illustration files along with some sage advice on how to recreate the book as a larger softcover second edition.

Since I already knew Photoshop, I used it to my advantage. I placed the rhyming verses onto each page of the beloved artwork and was surprised by how much fun it was. What began as a labor of love and necessity became a new skill. I redesigned the covers, removed the *Little Nuggets* logo, and added my new publishing imprint, Top Cat Publishing, on the back. By the time I uploaded the book to Amazon, I had the process down.

I then hired an illustrator for *Color Me Happy!*,

learned about storyboards, pacing, and how to build a picture book from the ground up.

At the same time, I began to look for a traditional publisher because I thought they might market it better than I could. I found Guardian Angel Publishing, a Christian children's book publisher that wanted both *Rainbow Nights* and *Color Me Happy!* Since *Color Me Happy!* was complete, I essentially handed them a finished product for their online bookstore.

Their company matched authors with illustrators and created the books at very little cost. Their income came from online sales and charging a bit more for author copies.

Guardian Angel paired me with illustrator Kit Grady for *Rainbow Nights*, and though I missed giving input on the artwork, the illustrations turned out beautifully. We were in sync on some deeper level, much like with *The Caterpillar's Dream*, when the artist somehow drew exactly what I had imagined.

Before long, my books were available online. But Guardian Angel Publishing wasn't doing much to promote my two new titles. I gave them a year, and when nothing happened, I decided to venture forth without a publisher.

It was a little frightening, but it felt good to regain control of my books. All three were back in my care, like runaway pets that had finally come home.

I reformatted everything under Top Cat Publishing just as I had done with *The Caterpillar's Dream*. With all the files in my hands and a growing confidence in my new skills, I created Kindle editions and even coloring books. I became a one-woman publishing house after all.

It was disappointing, of course, to see what had happened to my first book and the app. But as my own publisher, I was at peace. Susan was too. The book had already gone around the world and was still being read. The prophecy had been fulfilled.

Once I knew what I was doing, I could help others, too. Soon I was publishing their books and watching their dreams come true.

One of my favorite book projects was with an eighty-five-year-old PhD, a retired children's counselor. She shared a poem she had written about her little sister, who had died of influenza as a toddler.

"Can you really make a book with this, Sally?" JoAnn asked.

"I can," I told her. "I'll find the perfect illustrator, and you'll be amazed."

All her life, JoAnn had felt her sister nearby and called her Angel Betsy. I found a talented illustrator in Ukraine, and together we shaped her poem into a tender story.

When I placed *Adventures with Angel Betsy* in JoAnn's hands, her eyes filled with tears. Today, her granddaughter sells the little book in her store.

JoAnn is ninety-one now, and today she told me again how much it meant to her to have her book published. I gazed into her gentle eyes and knew it was true. She might have written a scholarly book with her PhD, but her children's story was dearest to her heart.

It mattered to Susan too, to see JoAnn's book find its way into the world. Maybe that's what pulls me toward helping others. Because everyone has a story.

28

INTO THE ARTS

I stayed in dentistry and helped others publish when they crossed my path. I poured my remaining time into writing and embraced the longevity of this lifetime compared to Susan's. I've never taken the gift of time for granted, and that perspective found its way into this poem.

Mid-life is
the afternoon
you'd better hurry
for soon night falls.

Youth is spent.
Choices fade
like smoke in the wind;
life is a half-eaten chocolate cake.

The tempo quickens.
Where is love?
Sift the superficial
from the truth.

Forgive yourself
for precious time wasted.
Don't look back
there is no future in the past.

A reality check:
What have I accomplished?
What remains to do?
Thank God there's still time to dream.

With dreams tugging at my sleeve, I leaned into photography. We lived in a tourist destination, and our land was home to birds, bears, coyotes, and the occasional cougar. Animals wandered through our backyard every day. In the place we called home, we were the visitors. The nearby Olympic Mountains blushed at sunrise, eagles glided overhead, and every season arrived with its own palette of colors. What was better than that?

I joined the local camera club to become a better photographer, unaware of what photography clubs were really like. Suddenly I was showing my images on a giant screen while a judge gave them a thorough critique in front of fifty pairs of eyes. Uncomfortable as it was, those comments were gold.

My health during those years was always shaky, but I showed up. The club became my anchor. I never talked about my health. Everyone had their own story. Some members were young and jetting around the world for photos. Others were pushing ninety, arriving at a meeting with a walker and a smile. None of it mattered. We had a camaraderie.

Early on, I entered a white peony photo in the club's competition, and to my amazement, it won first place. I was sitting next to Jim Martin, a longtime member and respected PSA judge with the presence of a kindly Santa Claus. When my image appeared on the screen, he leaned over and whispered, "You're the best photographer here, Sally."

I didn't expect praise like that, and it was the first time I wondered if maybe I really had a gift. I came from a family of photographers and artists, and perhaps the gift was so natural I didn't see it at first.

To this day, when I lift my camera, I think of Jim and the confidence he had in me long before I had it myself. I'm grateful for the members who lit the path, teaching me how to see, compose, and edit. I didn't realize it then, but they were also teaching me how to mentor others. It was real hands-on learning, the foundation no online course could give me. I rubbed elbows and tripods with some of the most talented photographers I'd ever met.

In time, I became a bird photographer, eventually earning the nickname the "Bird Whisperer" from my fellow phototogs. Did I really love birds? At first, I only knew a handful of their names. What drew me in, I have to admit, was discovering that birds were the most challenging subject of all. So, of course, I thought, *Well, that's for me!*

With over 350 species on the Olympic Peninsula, it became my goal to photograph both sexes of as many as I could. And then something unexpected happened. I fell in love with them.

The birds became more than subjects in my viewfinder. They shaped my days and my stories, which delighted Susan. I say Susan, but we were so integrated that all I could feel was her love for nature. Through my experiences with the birds, she was living in the Now, enjoying a life she never had the chance to experience in England. There were no cameras with zoom lenses back then, for one thing.

Each encounter taught me something. Some moments were funny, some surprising, and others touched me so deeply I carried them home like treasures. Bird photography stretched me as an artist, too. I learned to read light in an instant, to wait far longer than I thought I could, and to celebrate the single sharp frame hiding inside a hundred blurry ones.

It connected me with people as well. Friends in the camera club wanted to hear about my latest sightings, and strangers online began following my images with genuine excitement.

And somewhere in the waiting and watching, I healed. The steadiness of bird photography, the quiet, the air, and the sense of presence gave my spirit room to breathe. Being with the birds brought me back to myself in a way I hadn't expected, and I was grateful for every moment they allowed me to witness.

I joined the local Audubon group and started presenting my photos there. They had some remarkable photographers, yet their belief was simple: protect the bird, and the photograph will follow. That was exactly how I felt. The birds weren't just subjects; they were beings I was privileged to witness. Bird photography became the best kind of addiction. The call to rise early in the morning, to hear the first bird songs of the day, and to be there as a silent observer.

A Little Bit of Crazy

On a snowy winter morn
Before the rising sun and songs of birds,
While others slumber and coffee brews,
Something supersedes breakfast,
Comfort and climate
A call
To capture in digital detail
Nature's awakening.

There is a little bit of crazy
In those crack of dawn photographers
With bed head hair,
Layers of mismatched clothing,
Wool caps, fingerless gloves
Easing winter's bite.

Scanning the horizon, listening,
With thoughts of light and shutter speed,
Stealthy, determined, alert creatures
With rosy frozen faces
Lugging hefty telephoto lenses.

We tell ourselves
It is all worth it
Crazy is underrated!

29

IT'S ALL LOVE

My own story continued. I had integrated Susan into my life as best I could, though the process was anything but simple. In the early years after recognizing her as me, I was caught between two eras, living in the present moment, yet visited by visions and memories from another century and country.

Today, Susan seems to go along for the ride, content and almost amused that she has lived this long and experienced so much.

When I nearly died in 2017, the boundary between Susan's world and mine dissolved. I realized a deeper truth I had known before: that Soul endures, and love is what carries us forward.

A medical intuitive had warned me that my body was clotting abnormally, and tests eventually confirmed it. I had been getting scans for years, and one day they found clots in both legs. I remember the look on the technician's face.

"You need to go straight to the ER," she said.

In the ER, I tried to stay calm as the doctor explained what would happen next. "We're going to do a CT scan to see if there are any clots in your lungs."

I was fine until they came back with the results. There were no clots in my lungs, but they had found a mass in my appendix, and that scared me more than anything.

I remembered an odd sensation in my right abdomen months before. It was a strange feeling, almost like a warning signal, and then it went away.

"We need to do appendix surgery," the doctor said.

I must have turned white, because the nurse came in and gave me a drug for shock.

Everything moved quickly after that. Three days later, I was in pre-op for a high-risk surgery. Surgeons prefer not to operate when blood clots are present.

They put a cap on my head and wheeled me into a tiny room with the door closed. I lay there by myself, thinking, I don't belong here. I'm a nature photographer and a writer, not someone on a cot waiting to be cut open. Then another thought surfaced, the practical voice I have learned to trust: Be grateful they caught it in time.

Just then, a doctor I'd never met walked in with a chart in his hand.

"Hello, Susan. I'm your anesthesiologist. It's good to meet you."

"I'm Sally..." I barely managed to say. The moment he spoke my past-life name, I knew this was no accident. It was a sign that I was not alone, that someone had sent him to watch over me. His eyes twinkled, then softened with a loving concern I can still picture today.

"I rarely offer this to my patients," he said quietly, "but I wondered if you would like me to say a prayer now."

I nodded. "Yes. Thank you so much."

"Dear Lord..." he began. His prayer wrapped around me like a warm blanket. It touched my heart and gave me the strength I needed for what was coming next.

They wheeled me into the operating room, bright and cold, filled with stainless steel and trays of instruments. I remember the lights above me and the blur of masked faces. My last thought before going under was a simple prayer of my own: Please let me come back. I still have things to do.

When I woke up, I was weaker than I had ever been, but alive. The next day, the anesthesiologist stopped by my room.

"I just wanted to say hello and see how you are. Take good care of yourself," he said, then slipped away.

I didn't know if anesthesiologists usually visit their patients afterward, but his kindness stayed with me.

Five days later, I was home. My doctor told me I had

dodged two silver bullets. I knew I had. There are details of that experience better left unsaid, but the most important part of it all is not the fear or the medical facts. It's the love.

I was weak, with a seven-inch incision where they had removed a cancerous appendix. My body moved slowly, but my inner world was filled with rolling waves of love. It came from everywhere: Al's steady presence, my family and friends holding me in their prayers, and a deeper current from the inner worlds that I had known before, but never so clearly.

As I lay in bed recovering, all the layers of my life, past and present, folded into one another. What remained was the purest essence of me as Soul.

For days I was physically helpless, yet completely calm. Waves of love washed over me and through me, softening and strengthening everything I was and everything I knew. Language falls short when describing a love like that.

I sensed our true home, the place where we are Love itself.

I had come close to leaving this world, but I woke after surgery with a deeper understanding of why I'm here. My purpose was simple: to give love, to receive love, and to recognize it as the golden thread that connects all life.

That awareness shaped all that came next.

Everything mattered more, even the small things I once rushed past. I learned to listen to my body in a way

I never had before. It spoke clearly now, sometimes firmly, sometimes in a whisper. When it said *enough,* I paid attention. When it said rest, I listened.

I photographed differently, too. I lingered longer and waited without urgency. Birds taught me that. Instead of forcing a moment, they trust timing, instinct, and stillness. And I learned to do the same.

I had been given the grace of time, and I was on a mission. I tuned into the cycles of nature. While the world was still sleeping and the mornings were fresh with dew and possibility, I gathered my camera gear to capture the greatest show on earth.

Sunrise Mission

Just in time
For the morning show
Velvet fog fades with the rising sun
Golden rays
Shoot from the fireball
And shimmer across the bay
Gulls cry out their high-pitched
"Scree! Scree!"
Dipping and circling
Riding the winds of change
I dare to walk alone
With a camera, a hat, and frozen fingers
Lost in "the zone"
Zooming in, tracking the loveliness

Rapid-fire shots
Moments are captured
Digitalized, printed and framed
To bring you along
Breathe salt air
Make footprints in wet sand
Pocket an agate and a clam shell
As waves pound the shoreline
In perfect rhythm.

The past stopped pulling at me, because Susan had found her place. She was no longer a mystery to solve, but a companion walking alongside me.

Love continued to arrive. Not in grand gestures, but steadily, through the friendship of animals and the unspoken kindness of strangers.

30

IVORY

The bird's name was Ivory, and that's all I knew about the white peacock. He'd ended up at the Olympic Game Farm in Sequim.

I'd seen a photo of Ivory on Facebook – a black-and-white image taken by a friend. He was breathtaking, simple, and pure. I'd never seen a white peacock before and didn't know they existed. But I knew I had to meet that bird.

It was the beginning of COVID-19, and just days before the total shutdown of non-essential businesses.

Officials had already advised the public to stay home, but the game farm remained open. I headed out there and found an empty parking lot. The change in human behavior was obvious. People were afraid to venture out in public, and the emptiness was eerie.

I had the place to myself.

No sooner had I parked my car than the white

peacock strutted through the open entry gate to greet me and paused at a safe distance to eyeball my actions. I grabbed my Nikon, and slowly emerged from the car. As a bird photographer, I knew how to approach birds, so I stood and waited. He seemed amused by my hesitancy, but I sensed his invitation to get closer.

You know when you're having a magical moment. The present is alive, and you are completely here. All your senses are focused and receptive.

I breathed in gratitude and raised my camera. As I did, the peacock responded. He began a little dance, pivoting and shaking his silky feathers ever so slightly, watching my reactions. The beauty mesmerized me, and love flowed into me as if I'd been dehydrated.

Weeks of alarming news and confusing media reports had captured my attention. The world was changing fast. How could I be standing in front of nature at its finest when the rest of the world was in a tailspin?

I crept a few steps closer. The sky was a bit dark, so I adjusted my camera settings. Photographing white feathers on a sunny day burns out detail. It's always a balancing act, paying attention to the tech side while connecting to your subject. And with birds, you need to be quick!

Click, click, click. Close-up head shot, side view, full body shot. The peacock was performing for me, turning round and round so I could see the full package, playing to the camera like a professional model. Six feet of tail feathers swished behind him. Then he stopped, tilted his head back, and opened his beak. "Kaay-YOW, kaay-YOW, kaay-YOW!" I got a good look at the spiky palate inside his pink mouth. It was going to be a great shot!

He finished his call and stood facing me. All was still as he peered into my eyes. This is what I live for; I call it being in the zone, when we connect soul to soul, and the rest of the world melts away.

What happened next is hard to put into words. It was unexpected and magnificent. He opened his iridescent white tail feathers into a glorious fan, like an offering to me. His train of feathers was now a huge half-moon surrounding his pretty little head. This was the grand finale. He shimmied to the beat of his own music, setting the tips of the long feathers swaying. As I clicked the shutter, I whispered, *thank you, thank you.* In full display, he turned round and round, making sure I saw everything. When it was time, and the love and tranquility I had thirsted for had been replenished, he folded his white feathers and trotted off.

31

WINTER'S GIFT

Soul is the software
that slips into the hardware
at birth.
A perfect union,
powered by
the omnipresent Universal Server.
A full-service plan,
granted by grace
and extending until
mission fulfilled.

At the end of a life, when the burden becomes too heavy for the body to carry, it finally says, "I'm done." And then we go on to our heavenly home, where all is well. As the old hymn says, *It Is Well with My Soul.*

If there is one thing, or many things, I have not completed here, I have no concern. Susan has taught me that life is eternal, and that earthly incarnations are simply successive chapters of eternity, chapters I can barely comprehend.

Even as I write these words, I recognize how little I truly know. I do not claim certainty. What I have seen for myself feels like a fleeting glimpse, like being a passenger on a speeding locomotive, looking out the window as the scenery rushes past. In this conscious state, I have seen only what is mine to see, what I am meant to witness and understand at this level of awareness.

I wrote these pages mostly to do something while waiting for my fractured back to heal. I had put off writing the Susan story long enough. I simply hoped to have something to show for the weeks that turned into months, when so much of my life stood still.

I could stand at the computer when I couldn't sit, and even with a pinched nerve in my shoulder, I could type carefully if I took my time. Each day, I made myself a cup of tea and petted my black Siamese cat, who rested quietly on my office chair.

In the mornings, I kissed my husband goodbye as he walked out the door to play pickleball, a game I once played myself, until my body filed a formal complaint. I will not pretend that was easy. There were moments of envy for his pain-free, athletic body and for his ability to move in ways I no longer could. That's where I get into trouble: when I look around and notice what I do not have, or compare myself to what I used to do.

So I adapted, finding ways to keep going that fit the body I have now. First on the list was using lightweight camera gear and avoiding photographing birds in thirteen-degree weather on slippery ice.

In writing this book, I revisited the past and relived emotions. It was easy to get swept out to sea by some of my feelings. They were like well-worn pieces of forgotten fabric that I sewed into a patchwork quilt. Some were the soft pink of a baby's blanket. Others were garish and jolting, like rough burlap dyed blood-red. Yet together they made something beautiful, a life well-lived.

I set out to create a timeline, a sequence of a woman's journey, integrating her past-life self into today, a soul-thread woven through time.

To assist in my research, I put together a scrapbook of my writing, filled with newspaper articles and magazine copies. And why stop there? I boxed up all my photography award ribbons, stared at them and asked myself, *What does all this mean?*

For Susan, it meant I got to complete what I couldn't finish in nineteenth-century England. It was about eternity.

It was like little Nathan, returning to Earth to re-experience flying after being a pilot in World War II.

Then I began counting my blessings instead of blue ribbons.

Winter's Gift

Aged fingers trace
crystalline patterns of window frost
as cotton-candy snowflakes
dance upon the wind.

Like snow-covered trees,
she rests in well-earned dormancy.
A lifetime of seeds has been planted
to bloom in latter days.

A snowy down comforter
blankets the earth,
tucking it in
for a season's repose.

She stands alone
on her old wooden porch,
beholding winter's gift,
timeless white frosting,
a Christmas card portrait
of pristine innocence.

The hush of infinity
frozen in place.

In the stillness of the moment
she touches the eternal,
and her heart remembers
serenity.

ABOUT THE AUTHOR

Sally M. Harris is a Pacific Northwest award-winning photographer and author.

She has published short stories, children's books and poetry. Inspiration comes through dreams and time spent in nature. Her intention is simple: to open hearts with words, stories, and images.

When you see Sally out in nature, she is usually carrying a long lens and tripod, dressed in camo green. She spends hours waiting—watching and listening—often writing stories to accompany her bird encounters.

Her photography has appeared in many books and publications, including *Birds & Blooms* magazine.

IF YOU ENJOYED THIS BOOK

If *Susan Within: When a Past Life Returns* touched your life in some way, I would be grateful if you would leave a brief review.

Sharing your thoughts helps other readers discover the book and encourages conversations about the experiences and questions explored in its pages.

Thank you for taking this journey with me.

— Sally M. Harris

CONTINUE THE JOURNEY

Visit **SusanWithin.com** to:

- Contact me
- Join the *Susan Within: Sharing Spiritual Journeys* Facebook group—a welcoming space to share stories, synchronicities, dreams, spiritual insights, and life experiences.

Scan the QR code below to visit the website.

BOOKS BY SALLY M. HARRIS

POETRY

Another Springtime: The Poetry of Life

CHILDREN'S BOOKS

The Caterpillar's Dream

The Caterpillar's Dream Coloring Book

Color Me Happy!

Color Me Happy Coloring Book

Rainbow Nights: Dreamtime Fun!

Made in United States
Troutdale, OR
07/09/2026

50864520R00100